# NETWORKING FOR NOVICES

### NETWORKING NUGGETS FROM EXPERTS TO TRANSFORM YOUR BUSINESS! TO TRANSFORM YOUR LIFE!

**DEBRA K. POPE**

Copyright© 2010 Debra K. Pope

Performance Publishing
McKinney, TX

All Worldwide Rights Reserved, McKinney, Texas

All rights reserved. No part of this publication may be reproduced, stored in a retrieval system or transmitted in any form, or by any means, electronic, mechanical, recorded, photocopied, or otherwise, without the prior permission of the copyright owner, except by a reviewer, who may quote brief passages in review.

ISBN: 978-0-615-42489-7

www.NetworkingforNovices.com

Printed in Canada

# Table of Contents

Dedication ................................................................................... 6

Foreward .................................................................................... 7

Introduction ............................................................................... 9

Nugget #1 - Answering The "5 W" Questions About Networking ... 11

Nugget # 2 - Networking with a Plan and Purpose ...................... 17

Nugget #3 - Be Genuine, Be Yourself, Be Prepared ..................... 27

Nugget #4 – Your Image – Business and Personal ....................... 35

Nugget #5 – Your Business Card – Your Mini-Billboard ................ 61

Nugget #6 – Business Card Management ....................................... 65

Nugget #7 – Networking Etiquette ................................................ 69

Nugget #8 - Your Elevator Speech and Tag Line ........................... 75

Nugget #9 – Networking for Career Search or Career Advancement ................................................................................ 81

Nugget #10 - Public Relations Opens the Door to Successful Networking .................................................................................. 83

Nugget #11 - Building Relationships – "Giving First, Sharing Always" ........................................................................................ 95

Nugget #12 – Networking to Build Your Database ..................... 107

Nugget #13 - Your Net Worth = Your Network .......................... 111

Nugget #14- Climbing The "Pyramid of Success" Against All Odds 119

Nugget #15 – Organizations to Join for Successful Networking ................................................................................ 127

Nugget #16 – Using Social Media for Networking ..................... 135

Nugget #17 - Achieving and Maintaining Good Health for Successful Networking ............................................................... 143

Nugget #18 – The Fortune is In the Follow Up .......................... 163

About the Author ..................................................................... 168

# Dedication

This book is dedicated to the lights of my life, our precious
children Lenda, Christopher, Rakel and Kelley,
and my wonderful husband, Paul.

Even with a magic wand and the ability to make a wish for the
most wonderful children and greatest husband in the world,
I couldn't have wished for more!

Paul, you are the love of my life and I continue to love you more
each day. Thank you for being the "Wings Beside My Wings!"

# Foreword

Depending on your understanding of what "networking" means, it's either a joyous experience that lifts you up or an awkward interaction that brings you down. My personal understanding of what I thought networking was 15 years ago left me empty and feeling like what I had to offer was not important or valued by others. I would attend "networking" events with expectations of getting new clients and promoting, at the time, my advertising agency. In actuality I found it very awkward to engage in conversations with strangers and, once I did, strike up a conversation, my focus was to get them to become a customer and "do" business with me. They, the prospects, were also focused on getting customers, so the dynamic between us was all about what we both "wanted" and our need to "get" something from each other.

Take this in for a moment. A room full of business professionals, hungry for new clients and business. All of us focused on what we are going to "get" from each other. No wonder I, along with most everyone else who attend networking mixers, often leave these events feeling empty or doubtful that our interactions will really turn into business. Really, even through you may have 10 or more business cards in hand for future follow-up, most of us do not follow up. When you do follow-up—after you have left 2,3, 6 messages with no reply—these potential new business leads drop off and the business card is retired to a stack of other business cards that you believe you will get back to later. Geez, I am worn out just thinking about this crazy cycle. We both know that those old business cards are never or rarely touched again. The truth of the matter is you probably have some business cards of dead people in your stack. I know I used, too.

With the advent of social media, like Facebook, networking has actually become worse for those wanting to sell or promote their business. While we are more connected than ever, we are strangely more alone!

Business people thought that Facebook and Twitter would be huge booms for their businesses, helping them "get" more business.
The truth is no one wants to be "sold" anything through their social media networks. Selling through social media is like selling someone during dinner

on a cruise ship or in the line to purchase a movie ticket. For heaven's sake, you proclaim, "I'm trying to enjoy myself here, don't sell to me now!" There is a reason it's called "social" media. It's about being friendly, not pitchy.

So what's a smart savvy person to do? How do you increase your profits and gain access to the resources you need? How do you network in a way that you can be successful? How can you attract customers to you like a magnet? How can you get potential customers to pay attention to you and what you have to offer?

I have good news for you!

You have in your hands right now the answers to all of those questions. This book, Networking for Novices, will transform your business and your life if you are ready to learn and incorporate these teachings into the fiber of your being.

Debra Pope is the living embodiment of everything taught in this powerful book. What I so admire about Debra is her compassion to help others and provide the coaching and proven insights that have helped her propel her life forward. What Debra shares, along with the experts she has hand selected to feature in this transformational book, are proven strategies and ideas that work!

About 15 years ago I had no idea how to be successful at networking. By learning how to network, as outlined in this book, I am today the president of one of the most successful women's business networks in North America, eWomenNetwork. Through the power of networking, I became the executive producer of the critically-acclaimed movie: The GLOW Project and the co-founder of the dynamic new social media community called MyGLOW.net.

Take in this book and prepare yourself for big things. Networking works when you "work it" the right way. It is a joyous experience and Networking for Novices shows you the way.

**Kym Yancey**
**Co-Founder & President, eWomenNetwork**
**Executive Producer: The GLOW Project**
**Co-Founder: MyGLOW.Net**

# Introduction

If you are a student in school or graduating soon, an entrepreneur, small business owner, large business owner, corporate executive, new to the business world, seeking to climb the corporate ladder, re-enter the job market, looking for a job or career change or in any other walk of life , you need *networking*.

When I interviewed people I know for this book to learn their Networking techniques and skills, many gave me the answer: **"I'm not in sales, so I don't need *networking*."**

This answer came from people in a variety of fields and from various walks of life. The answer **"I don't need *networking*"** has been given to me by a doctor, a lawyer, an accountant, a teacher, a student and a pastor. Yet, I've known people in these very professions who successfully built their practices and careers with successful, intentional *networking*.

You may be thinking that **you** don't need nor have the time for *Networking*. Before you make a definitive decision that you don't need *networking*, read this book.

My goal, and the goal of the "*Networking* Experts" in this book, is to give you the tools you need to make *networking* a positive, planned, intentional, focused and productive activity.

*Networking* can and should be one of the most critical and rewarding tools in your arsenal of promoting you and your business.

This book is a guide to focused, intentional, prepared, efficient ***networking***.

We've all heard these old adages:

"Time is money" and "You only have one chance to make a first impression."

This book is a guide on how to maximize your time and money to your best advantage.

This guide provides a common-sense approach and sure-fire way to spread the word about your fabulous product and service.

I've spent years perfecting the craft of *networking*. In this book, *Networking for Novices*, I've gathered together the best of the best professionals who have a long and effective history of utilizing *networking* to spread their message about the products and services they offer.

This guide provides hints, tips, ideas and plans for successful *networking*. Take advantage of the experience we, the authors of *Networking for Novices*, have compiled to save you the time and the money we've expended in getting this experience.

Read on, and we know you will be pleasantly surprised to learn from those of us who regularly use and love Networking for friendships, relationships, client introduction, resources, marketing and products or services they need. Reading this book will help you make a plan, focus, develop intentional relationship building, increase your net worth and your network, and have an enjoyable time doing it!

Small business is the fuel that fires the engine of the American economy. We want you to succeed. You owe it to yourself, the future of your family and the future of your country to succeed!

I wish you the greatest of success! I look forward to seeing you soon at a *networking* event!

Debra K. Pope
And the Contributing Authors of
***Networking for Novices***

# NUGGET #1

## Answering The 5 "W" Questions Of *Networking*.

There are 5 critical questions that need to be answered by people before they use the tool of Networking to promote themselves and their businesses. **The 5 Questions are**:

1. What is Networking?
2. Who needs Networking?
3. Why do I need Networking?
4. When do I do Networking?
5. Where do I go to do Networking?

<u>Answer to Question #1</u>: **What is *networking*?**

The definition of *networking* in the Encarta Dictionary is the "practice of gathering of contacts." A further definition is "the process or practice of building up or maintaining informal relationships, especially with people whose friendship could bring advantages, such as job or business opportunities."

The definition of *networking* in the Reference World Online Encyclopedia as a noun comes in two parts: 1) the exchange of information or services among individuals, groups or institutions, or the cultivation of productive relationships for employment or business.

Answer to Question #2: **Who needs *networking*?**

The answer is **everyone in every type of business, every age group and every stage of business and life needs *networking*.**

As part of your marketing and sales plan, *networking* is a vital and necessary component of a successful business plan.

Answer to Question #3: **Why do I need *networking*?**

In good or bad economic times, *networking* is the most effective and lowest-cost method of spreading your message.

The biggest obstacle facing businesses, small or large, is public awareness of the existence of their product or service.

Few businesses have the budget to carry out a large advertising campaign in print, radio or television with enough frequency and fanfare to gain mainstream awareness of their products and services.

Small business people, of whom I'm one, find that marketing and advertising for their company in traditional radio, television, print and direct mail formats is an expensive and inexact science at best.

How do you know what radio station, which television station, which newspaper and what form and method of direct mail will be most effective for your business? How do you know what frequency and schedule you will need for the ads you use?

The only sure-fire way to find out if a particular advertising medium will work for you and your company is to do it. Try it to see if it works, but this is extremely expensive and time-consuming.

You must have an effective tracking method to see if it has worked, which takes more time and money.

Tracking of advertising's effectiveness is difficult to do with any degree of certainty. The rule of thumb is that consumers must see and hear your advertisement consistently at least seven times before they act on your invitation to do business with you.

In my 25 years of small business ownership, I've spent over $1,000,000 dollars on marketing and advertising!

I'd like an opportunity for a "do-over" and be able get that money back!

As a fellow small business person, I care about you and your business. I recommend you carefully analyze your product and service and who your target market is before committing to radio, television, print or other direct mail options.

**When you sporadically and blindly place ads in print, radio, television and direct mail, you are <u>throwing money at the problem</u>** as the answer to your advertising and marketing questions.

Many business people make the mistake of arbitrarily placing ads in "traditional" methods of advertising, such as in local newspapers and magazines, marketing materials like cups, pens, coupons, and cable and television, based on the **advice given to them by the salesperson selling the ads.**

While there is a place for traditional methods of advertising, many small business people use them, **and never consider or give very little thought to** *networking* as being a necessary and valuable component of their plan for Marketing and Sales.

<u>Answer to Question #4:</u> **When do I do Networking?**

The answer is: **Now is the time to do** *networking*.

**Cutting back on** *networking* **in a slower economy is the biggest mistake a business can make!** I hear people saying we're cutting back on *networking* because of the slow economy. Or, "We need to wait to do *networking* until the economy turns around to keep our costs down." I'm shocked when I hear that excuse! Networking **now** is the best way to promote you and your business, in a booming economy or a slow economy.

In a "slower or sluggish economy," you should be *networking* more than ever, reaching out to more of your potential clients more than ever!

Do the arithmetic. If you participate in one event a month it can cost from $25-$50, depending on where you live. What effective marketing strategy can you produce for $50 or less? There really isn't much else you can do for that amount AND get fantastic results.

Let's talk about the economy. Do you, a business owner or executive, really not have $25-$50 to spend to meet 8 to 10 new prospective clients? That's the number of new people you usually will have time to meet in a 2 to 3 hour *networking* event. If that's actually the case, then perhaps this is the time to re-examine your marketing strategies and determine where you are getting the most bang for your buck.

The truth is—you certainly cannot stop marketing just because times are tough. *Networking* is the least expensive, most cost-effective way to market and advertise your business.

While you're trying to save money, you're costing your business big time. The most important aspect of running a business is keeping your name out there. Great employees, quality control, customer service, expertise, experience, innovative products and services—they're all extremely important, but they're meaningless if nobody knows about you.

Instead of foolishly keeping yourself in your office thinking, "We're not spending any money right now, until we get through this," think about what your questionable marketing savings plan is doing to your business.

Years ago in New Jersey, the NJ Dental Association ran a very successful billboard campaign throughout the state: "Ignore your teeth and they'll go away." Well, to paraphrase: **ignore your business and it will go away**.

Now is the time to position yourself and your company away from all the conventional thinkers who are feeling sorry for themselves and show your smiling face and your confident outlook. Now is the time to maintain client relationships and build alliances. Now is the time to show the world that you refuse to participate in the recession (thank you, Sam Walton).

**You must learn how to be a savvy networker – how to really connect with others – and how to follow up.** Simply going to *networking* events without a plan will bring you very few of the results you'd like to have. Through this book, you have the opportunity to learn these strategies and put them into practice at your local *networking* events.

Don't miss out on networking opportunities through misguided thinking about "cost." Networking is low in cost and it can become the best money you ever spend – if you know how to "make it work!"

The country will get through all the economic uncertainty, just as we always come through. To have a head start on your competition, now is the time to do Networking! Cutting back on crucial marketing that costs $50 or less is not the way to save money.

Answer to Question #5: **Where do I go to do Networking?**

A comprehensive list of what organizations to join or attend for successful, purposeful networking is Nugget #15. Here is the short list:

> Your Local Chamber of Commerce
> Charity or Non-Profit Events
> eWomenNetwork
> Business Networking International
> Service Organizations such as Rotary, Lions, or Kiwanis.

**Networking is the ANSWER! It is the most efficient, thorough and cost-effective answer to promote you and your business in a good economy or a slower economy.**

**Read and utilize *Networking for Novices* to make the best use of your time and investment in Networking.**

# NUGGET #2

## *Networking* With A Plan & Purpose

### Introduction by Debra K. Pope

It's not wise to start a journey without a map. Neither is it wise to begin a journey without a plan that includes what mode of transportation you will take, how you will travel, which direction you are headed and how long it will take you to get there. Neither is it wise to promote you, your company, your service and your products without a business plan. Your business plan should include Networking.

Now, I'd like to introduce you to one of the most effective experienced and adept Networkers, I know, Saralyn Collins. She has taught hundreds of people in her sales training classes to apply Outcome-Based Thinking. I've had the pleasure of being taught by Saralyn on goal setting, time management, sales and marketing, all with the plan of Outcome-Based Thinking.

Following is Saralyn's guide to Networking utilizing Outcome-Based Thinking.

Saralyn Collins is owner of The Training Bridge and a seasoned Certified Marketing Consultant, Executive Trainer and Franklin Covey Coach.

Saralyn's 30+ years of experience have provided a unique ability to design solutions for business growth. From helping develop two multi-million dollar direct sales companies to training throughout the US with the International Guild of Professional Consultants, then as Executive Director of Training for eWomenNetwork, providing strategies for personal and professional growth to thousands of businesswomen for over 6 years, she continued to grow The Training Bridge into a powerful resource for anyone who wants to become a "business magnet!"

Saralyn and her husband, Marshall, alternate their time between Orlando, FL and Asheville, NC, where they get to babysit their grandson, Jackson.

**Saralyn Collins**
consultantsc@cfl.rr.com
www.TheTrainingBridge.com
www.comF5.com/trainingbridge

407-644-6538 FL Office
407-421-5628 cell
828-469-8011 NC office

# Networking With A Plan & Purpose

By Saralyn Collins

*"I'm never going back to that networking group again. I didn't get anything out of it! It's just a waste of my time and money."*

How many times have I heard a woman say that after attending a *networking* event—one I found to be productive, enjoyable, and certainly worth attending again? Well, the answer is—entirely too many times. Of course, I want to grab her by the shoulders, give her a good shake, and ask, "You didn't GET anything? So, what did you GIVE? Have you thought about that?"

You have opened a book to learn how to be a more effective networker - to transform your business and your life. It can happen. *Networking* can become one of the most powerful marketing strategies you have at your disposal. Network novice or not, you are in the right place if you can learn the purpose of *networking* and how to get results!

*Networking* can be time-consuming but it can also produce amazing results. It can be somewhat expensive at times but the return on investment is amazing. It can certainly exhaust yet revitalize you at the same time.

Many people engage in *networking* activities on a regular basis. Why do so many still complain about it and, more importantly, why do so many never see a good return on that investment of time, money, and energy?

After over thirty-years of using *networking* as a productive and rewarding strategy to build name recognition and brand awareness, I think I know the problem! It starts at the very beginning of the entire process. Throughout this book you will be introduced to amazing strategies that bring value and add power to your *networking*.

In his excellent book, *Rainmaking: The Professional's Guide to Attracting New Clients,* Ford Harding makes the following observation: "*Networking* is one of the most referenced and seldom realized activities in business…I suspect more time is wasted on so-called networking than on any other area of the professional services. This is disturbing, because the value of time spent on marketing far exceeds the value of out-of-pocket expenses in most firms." He goes on to list fourteen basic rules for effective *networking*, many of which are common guidelines and will be discussed in the remainder of this book.

**STEP ONE: The Purpose**

I am a strong believer in a concept called "outcome-based thinking": you determine various outcomes you must have if you are going to spend time and energy on that activity. Let's talk about this process for a minute, because it can bring about distinct changes in the results you get.

I have always believed if I knew the *purpose*, or the *why*, of something, I would understand how to act and what to do in the future. It is important to understand the true purpose of *networking*, and guess what? It may not be what you think!

From a purely professional aspect, the purposes of *networking* are:

1. Build your name recognition in your community
2. Build awareness and value of your expertise
3. Have prospects seek you out and want to know more about you and your business

Let's examine each one of these so we can set our outcomes appropriately.

**1. Build your name recognition in your community**

Over the years, we have shifted our understanding of marketing and what it is supposed to accomplish for us. We have shifted from "promoting" to "positioning." This means simply, you perform activities that position you in front of people so you can become known. You get involved in organizations or charities where your target market is likely to be present.

If you take it at face value, you might be tempted to think of it as manipulative, but I'm not suggesting you get involved in any group where you do not see value and purpose in the organization. If you decide to get involved in a charity, it has to be one in whose cause you believe and want to promote. If you get involved in an organization, you should agree with its purpose and vision so you can promote value.

The purpose of this strategy is to "position" you in places of leadership, so that others become aware of you as an individual who knows how to bring value to whatever you do. Get on an active committee, where you can show your ability to produce "results." You want to show everyone that you know how to take responsibility and produce a great result!

When your target market sees you involved and giving back, volunteering your time and energy on something important to them, that tells them something about you personally. They now see you as more than just your business; they see you for a good human being who gives back to the community.

Don't do this if you aren't going to take it seriously. By that I mean actually DO the work required by being on that committee. If you can become the "chair," do all the reporting and public representation for that committee well. You want to be seen as someone who produces "results," no matter what you are doing.

This may be hard to believe, but here is the general understanding of how our minds work. If your target market prospect sees you producing "results" in a volunteer situation and you do an outstanding job, then the prospect's mind assumes, "Wow, if she did such a great job as a volunteer, how much better would she be if I pay her to work for me?" When you approach that prospect to talk about your services, you have already set the stage for how that individual thinks about you and what you are capable of doing.

There is no question that you need a reputation as one who is concerned about service to others. For nervous networkers, I often teach them a question to ask when they enter a room and don't know quite what to do next, but this question is great for anyone nervous or not:

"What do I need to know about you so I can easily recommend you to my friends and colleagues?"

By taking the emphasis off of what you can "get" from others and focusing on what you can "give" to them, you change the entire dynamics of an encounter.

Perhaps we should rightfully add a fourth purpose for *networking*: Discover others to whom you can be of service!

What a fantastic outcome for you to work toward: increasing the number of people you meet and to whom you can be of service. Without sounding cynical, this activity reinforces personal opinions about you and the value of what you offer when you work with someone.

### 2. Build awareness and value of your expertise

By carefully selecting the different activities you get involved in, you are also building awareness of your expertise as a professional person. This goes back to the first point – becoming known as someone who produces results.

When you can find areas of *networking* where you can use your expertise to help others, people become aware of you as a "specialist." Your outcome is to build awareness both of who you are as a person and what you offer as a business solution.

Your goal is to create "top of the mind" awareness, so when a prospect realizes he has a problem, you are the answer that pops to his mind first, and you popped into his mind because of all the work you have done in the past, the results you produced, and the relationships you have built.

By now you realize that accomplishment of both of these goals is not something that happens overnight. This is a process, and one that must be attended to over a period of time. Building name recognition and brand awareness simply takes consistent and well-structured time.

Those who have uttered the familiar, *"I went to that event and I got nothing out of it, so I am not going back"* should take a look at your strategy or lack thereof. Rarely will networking produce instant results but over time, it can do exactly what you need it to do: build your name recognition and move you to "top of mind" awareness so you can accomplish the final goal.

### 3. Have prospects seek you out and want to know more about you and your business

Here is your ultimate purpose for *networking*: The time, energy, and money you have put into *networking* of all types should ultimately produce valuable results. First, you want to instantly "come to mind" when someone has a business concern and tries to think of how she might get it solved. Secondly, you want to pop up first when someone does a "brain Google search."

If you have taken these seriously, and if you use all the "nuggets" in the rest of this book effectively, you will build name recognition and awareness of the value you produce. Colleagues will know who you are and what you do, and they will tell your story! Go into this strategy full force as long as you truly understand your purpose, which brings the value and guides your language and actions.

### STEP TWO: The Plan

A plan of action must always have growth goals for your business. Once you set those goals, you can design a plan of action around them. Planning is time-consuming, but you do it to actually save time and get better results.

Years ago, as I was grumbling about the need to get organized, my husband made a copy of the following quote from Stephen Brennan and hung it in front of my desk so I had to look at it every day:

> "Our goals can only be reached through the vehicle of a plan, in which we must fervently believe, and upon which we must vigorously act. There is no other route to success."

Let's assume that you understand and agree on the value of setting specific goals and that following through with a plan of action is important, and you are willing to give it a try.

You need to set some business growth goals. Once you set those goals, how do you implement them? How do you design your daily plan of action to accomplish those goals and grow your business?

A plan of action should include:

- What *networking* events in my area would be important for me to attend?
- How many can I work into my schedule effectively?
- What outcomes do I need for this to be a good use of my time?
- What specific business goals will this help me accomplish?
- What do I need to do to accomplish my goals?
- How do I prove the "value" of my product or service?

One of the first keys to accomplishing the steps in a plan of action is called "outcome-based thinking." Look at any activity or step in your plan and ask yourself all three of these questions:

1. What MUST I accomplish for this to be a worthy use of my time, energy, and money? Write down what you must accomplish.
2. "What SHOULD I accomplish if I just do what I know how to do? Write down these answers.
3. What COULD I accomplish if everything worked perfectly? Write down the best that could occur if everything fell into place and you got your fondest wishes for an outcome.

You need to specifically answer each of these questions, because once you know clearly your goals you can plan your language and actions to match those goals.

Why are you going to that specific *networking* event? My guess is that you have rarely, if ever, given thought to what you must accomplish when you are *networking*. This is why people spend time and money and get poor results.

I simply am not willing to trust my business future to "whatever" result might happen. I want to plan a clear outcome and then know how to get it. You can do this as well. It just takes a shift in your thinking and a little planning.

As you think through these outcomes, you often have to set up steps to take before the event in order to reach them. Maybe you have to plan your introduction, your "commercial," so that it makes a greater impact. (This is probably the greatest error we make when *networking*: an ineffective introduction.) Maybe you have to have the right materials to take with you. Think through everything you need to gain the optimum outcome.

As you plan all the different steps, you should be adding every step to your calendar so you are confident each is finalized before you attend. That means your chance of accomplishing your outcome is much greater.

My final questions to you are:

1. What do you want/need to accomplish when you use *networking* as a marketing strategy? Remember, each event or situation has different outcomes. Be specific.
2. What is your plan to accomplish these outcomes? Remember, language and action must be designed to deliver the desired outcome if you want the best results.
3. How are you going to handle all these new customers when you use *networking* with a plan and purpose? Wow! Won't that be an exciting problem to have?

By the time you finish this book, you will not only know the purpose and plan, you will know the exact steps you need to take so that you can network with power and for results!

# NUGGET #3

## Be Genuine, Be Yourself, Be Prepared

### Introduction by Debra Pope

To be genuine, you must be yourself. You first must be confident in who you are and have confidence in what you portray and what you represent. Few people reach success in an attempt to be something they are not.

I love old sayings. There are a few phrases out there that may seem to encourage you to be someone you are not, such as "Fake it until you make it."

My favorite saying sits on my desk: "Be brave. Even if you're not, pretend to be; no one can tell the difference."

Another of my favorites is "A broken clock is right twice a day." This saying encourages me to try to do my best, even in times of insecurity.

I encourage you to be genuine and confident, but always be "Others-focused." A saying that illustrates my conviction is "If you want to be more successful, you have to help more people."

To do so, you must also be prepared by doing your due diligence, or "doing your homework," to make sure you are ready when the opportunity arises for you to attend a *networking* event.

There is a woman you have to know who has shown me how to serve more people through her positive, uplifting message. She is one of the women whom I most admire and whose friendship I most treasure. She is Michelle Prince. She is an award winning author and coach, focusing on motivation and positive thinking. Through her speaking and coaching, she shares her positive, upbeat message of "Winning in Life Now" and of Living a Life of Passion and Purpose.

Without her care, encouragement and concern, the idea of *Networking for Novices* would have forever been just that–an idea, never put into print. Michelle saw the passion I have for promoting and connecting others and brought it out of me in a way no one else has.

Michelle has a knack for recognizing greatness in others, and believes in her clients, sometimes more than they believe in themselves.

Following is the insight of Michelle Prince for Nugget #3, how to "Be Genuine, Be Yourself, Be Prepared."

Michelle Prince is the Best-Selling Author of the book "*Winning in Life Now...How to Break Through to a Happier You!*" She has been endorsed by and worked for some of the most influential, successful motivational teachers and authors in the industry, including Zig Ziglar.

Michelle Prince has embraced personal development, goal-setting and the desire to improve her life since the age of 18. Michelle has taken that knowledge to transform not only her own life, but the lives of millions of people who want to break through to a life of greatness.

Aside from being an author, Michelle is a sought-after motivational speaker, one-on-on mentor and radio show host on the "Winning In Life Now Radio Show." She owns her own company, Prince Performance Group, as well as her own publishing company, Performance Publishing.

**Michelle Prince**
**Prince Performance Group**
**www.WinningInLifeNow.com**
**Info@PrincePerformance.com**

## Be Genuine, Be Yourself, Be Prepared

### By Michelle Prince

*Networking* is so much more than handing out business cards; it's about relationships. But no matter how good you are at building relationships, if you don't have one crucial quality within yourself, then your efforts to use *networking* to build your business will be fruitless.

In fact, without this quality you can't have any solid relationships at all. And without relationships, you can't build your business. If you can't build your business, then you can't live your dreams. What is this one quality? BELIEF!

Eighteen months ago I had a dream. My dream was to become a best-selling author and inspirational speaker and really make a difference in the lives of people all over the world.

The problem was, it was just a dream. I had no idea how to make it happen.

In July 2008, a good friend of mine was coming to Dallas to attend a personal development seminar. My friend had created a goals program that she sold at these seminars. Since my background had always been in sales, and she was a lifelong friend, I offered to come help her for three days to sell her products while she attended the conference. I had no way of knowing that this simple decision to help a friend would completely change my life.

At this time in my life, I was working a corporate job and living an ordinary life. I had greater aspirations for myself but I couldn't seem to get past my fears. Every time I allowed myself to dream about my future, my fears and self-doubt would seep in to convince me that not only was it not possible, but that I wasn't capable. I remained in this holding pattern for approximately eleven years.

I wish I knew then what I know now: how to let go of my fears and just go for it! I had, after all, worked for the "Master of Motivation," Zig Ziglar, early in my career. I had learned from Zig how to set goals and overcome obstacles, but somewhere along the way I forgot what I learned and gave into the temptation of thinking that happiness and success were for others and not me.

Why is it that so many of us adults give up on our dreams? Why was it so much easier to dream when we were kids? I'm sure you, like me, daydreamed of what you wanted to be when you were growing up. Back then, opportunities seemed endless and our dreams were all within our reach. However, somewhere along the way, many of us lost track of those dreams and the belief that we could do anything worthwhile.

Somewhere deep inside of you, there is still that kid living inside who knows what you really want out of life. It could be writing a book, starting a business, or taking that trip. The problem is, we push those dreams to the backs of our minds and minimize the importance of them because they seem too big or too bold. Before long, we forget about them altogether.

But if you just take the time to look within yourself and discover that passion again, you can dust off those dreams and put together a plan to go after them. It's only then that life starts to get really exciting. Trust me, I should know.

Since I worked for Zig Ziglar, I knew I loved personal development but I couldn't get my arms around how I could make a living in that area. After all, I wasn't a speaker or an author. In fact, I felt like I had nothing to offer in this area, so I continued down the path of just working for a living instead of living to work.

At one point in my life, I got honest with myself and thought about what I really wanted to be, do and have. I kept coming back to speaking and seminars and impacting people's lives like Zig Ziglar had for so many years. I wouldn't dare admit it to anyone, but my real goal was to be like Zig someday. Immediately, I'd catch myself and unconsciously think, "Who do you think you are? How dare you think you could ever measure up and be like Zig Ziglar? Get over yourself and get back to your normal life." And, so I did…until that day I decided to help my friend at her seminar.

I've always been inspired at seminars and being surrounded by other like-minded individuals who share my passion for personal development. That's not very typical of most people and certainly not of my neighbors, my family, or some of my good friends who were surrounding me at that time. But I light up when I'm at a seminar and when I'm around other people who are trying to better themselves, those who are motivated and want more for their life and have goals. I get fired up…and that's exactly what happened to me at this event.

I'm not sure if it was the timing of the seminar or a specific word spoken by one of the speakers, but something shifted in me that day. It was as if someone hit me over the head and I had that "a-ha" moment. For so many years, I'd been saying "Not me! Who am I to do this? I'm no Zig Ziglar!" I'd stop myself in my tracks and put myself down.

But on this day, I said to myself, "Why NOT me? I have a unique story to tell. I've gone through some situations that I believe people can relate to. I'm not perfect, but I've learned so many things through the years on how to improve myself, and I want to share this with people."

It finally occurred to me that if I had issues with my self esteem and goal setting even after working for Zig Ziglar all those years, then others might be struggling too. Maybe there are people who never even heard of goal setting and don't even know where to start. I could help them. So that's really what prompted me to go and do just that. It was like this light bulb just went off and I have never looked back since.

I really believe that in order to create a happy life, it boils down to belief–belief in yourself. You must believe that you can do something before you can even set out to do it. If you don't have the belief in yourself, you won't be able to accomplish anything.

We're all unique, we all have special gifts, we all have a purpose, and I believe it's our job to find that purpose and then live our lives fulfilling it. But so many of us are held back from these self-limiting beliefs, just like I was. They don't believe that they can accomplish their goals, so subconsciously they either sabotage their chance of success, or many just don't even bother trying.

You have to believe first in yourself in order for others to believe in you. People will usually treat you with the same amount of respect as you treat yourself. If you don't have the confidence that you can do a good job, then no one else is going to believe you can do it, either. It all starts with you.

So it took me a long time, but I finally figured out that my passion was to motivate, inspire and encourage others to live happier lives. I made a decision that day to follow my heart and to go after my goal. I literally went home from the seminar and began to write. Having never written before, I figured I'd have trouble, but the words flew out of me. I had the entire book written in three weeks. For someone who thought I had nothing to say, it was amazing to see how much had been in me for so long, just waiting to come out.

Fast-forward two years: I'm humbled and proud to say I am a best-selling author, sought-after motivational speaker, life mentor, radio host and happier than I've been in my entire life. And all of this was done while I was still working a full time job. It all started with a decision. It started with me taking a leap of faith and believing in myself.

I'm no different from you. I'm a wife, a mother, a daughter, a sister, just trying to do my best day in and day out, just like everybody else. But I am passionate about life, and I'm passionate about achieving my goals. And I've had that passion for a long, long time, and I just happen to have followed my dreams, which is why I'm sharing my story with you today.

What about you? What do you really want out of life? What dream do you have that you don't dare tell anyone or believe you can accomplish? If I can do it, so can you. Don't waste another moment delaying your dreams. Your life is so short and you are given only one chance to make it your best life, so why not go for it? If you believe that you can, then I know you will be able to accomplish big goals! I believe in you…and so does that kid deep inside you!

# NUGGET #4

## Your Image – Business & Personal

### Introduction by Debra Pope

We've all heard the old adage, "You only have one chance to make a good first impression." It's so important to make sure you put forth your best image. You want to do this every day, but especially when Networking. You want to "put your best foot forward" and to portray the very best image of you and your personal style to promote you and your business.

The lady I'm about to introduce to you is an expert in image, health and beauty. She has been in the image consulting field all her life. Her passion is enhancing the inner and outer beauty of her clients. She has formulated her own line of naturally based skin care products and cosmetics. Her approach to enhancing beauty is to promote health and wellness, inside and out.

She is a beautiful, caring woman who guides you through looking and feeling your best. Now, I'd like to introduce you to Helen Gibson-Nicholas.

Helen Gibson-Nicholas founded Hello Gorgeous Cosmetics in 1987. Her goal was to make an anti-aging skin care system that was not chemically laden with unsafe and sometimes carcinogenic ingredients. Her aloe skin care has been paraben- and glycol-free since the 80s; in fact her products were "green" before "green" became the buzz word for pure and natural, environmentally safe products.

Learn more about Helen and her 200% aloe vera anti-aging skin care, instructional videos, makeup and hair tips, fashion trends, mineral magic makeup, and much more at www.hellogorgeous.com. Or visit Hello Gorgeous in the new shopping complex located off Central Expressway and Stacy Road in the Allen/Fairview area of North Dallas: 111 Fountain Court, The Village At Fairview, 75069.

Helen is a Certified Image Consultant, Master Barber-Stylist, professional makeup artist, radio talk show host, author, and speaker. Helen is referred to as The Total Image Coach and has performed over 10,000 makeovers, helping women (and men) find their gorgeous potential. Finding your most flattering hairstyle, clothing and makeup colors, and makeup techniques reveal the confidence in the real you and gets you noticed. That's the gorgeous potential. Her motto: "I help you look like who you want to become."

**Helen Gibson-Nicholas**
**Hello Gorgeous Cosmetics, Inc**
**www.hellogorgeous.com**
**helen@hellogorgeous.com**

# Image Matters

### By Helen Gibson-Nicholas

I realized the importance of *networking* when I found myself starting over again at the age of 50. In 1997 our salon in Plano, Texas was going and growing. I had launched my skin care and cosmetics company a few years earlier, had a Saturday morning radio show that covered the DFW area, and was making several television appearances. Then, my husband decides he is just "burnt out" and wants to move back to our hometown in Louisiana.

I reopened Hello Gorgeous as a small cosmetic boutique in a quaint shopping village. Here I was again, starting from scratch. What's a girl to do? "Just do it!" I pushed up my sleeves and began *networking* in the Chamber of Commerce, a breakfast business exchange club, Rotary, several lunch groups, and a woman's Mardi Gras Krewe. I gave to every silent auction that asked and attended most of their balls or dinners.

It wasn't long before I moved to a larger location and opened a second location in a town across the river. We were honored with top ten small business of the year and received best spa/salon awards numerous times from the Shreveport Times, SB Magazine, and others. None of that would have happened if I just opened my door and simply waited for people to come. *Networking* works!

In *Networking For Novices* you will receive sound, proven information about *networking* and related matters. So what is my contribution? Since they call me "The Total Image Coach," "My Beauty Coach," and "The Health and Beauty Babe," it doesn't take a rocket scientist to know I'm going to talk to you about your image. I want to help you understand how your image affects others. I will convince you that image matters. Do you remember the camera commercial that proclaimed "Image is everything"? OK, they were talking about the picture that is produced, but the phrase is so right on. You will be amazed to learn image is an aspect of your success that cannot be over-looked, skimped on, or dismissed.

You may think you are selling shoes, jewelry, real estate, business planning, or insurance, but you are not. You are selling you, and you only get one chance to make a good first impression. In fact, within three seconds we silently decide whether we want to continue a conversation. A whopping 93% of communication comes from how you look and sound, not what you are saying. It breaks down like this:

- 55% is based on appearance
- 38% is based on vocal expression
- 7% is based on actual words

You can see that no matter how great the sales presentation or sales pitch, people have already decided who you are from your image. When you start talking, even though you make perfect sense, it may not have an impact at all if those listening do not like your visual and vocal presence. From the moment you are in view, make the most of those few seconds, because first impressions are lasting impressions. Your visual impact must correspond with actual skills and knowledge of your field. Someone once said, "Why not package yourself to show what you know, from the word go?"

What is your image saying? Image professionals know that image is about establishing an impression. Certified Image Professional Ann Reinten says, "Image is all about establishing a deliberate and favorable impression to assist others to believe the evidence of what they see. If you present yourself visually and behaviorally as a successful person, others will respond to you accordingly."

Image comes from three things:

1) **How you look**
2) **How you act**
3) **How you think**

**HOW YOU LOOK**

Let's explore how you look first. I came across an impressive survey done in 2001 by The Cosmetic, Toiletry, and Fragrance

Association and Women Work! (the National Network for Women's Employment) that found 69% of most Americans believe clothing, hair, and makeup are very important or extremely important for a woman to make a good impression on the job. Only 7% believe it is not very or not at all important. The findings on whether Americans believe a woman's appearance at work affects certain aspects of her future performance on the job were as follows:

- 84% believe it affects her ability to represent her company in outside meetings
- 76% believe it affects her being taken seriously
- 74% believe it affects her being asked to participate in meetings with upper management
- 67% believe it will determine her being given new challenges, responsibilities, and opportunities
- 64% believe appearance is considered for a raise or promotion
- 46% believe it affects confidence
- 59% believe it affects her ability to perform her job

What about hair and makeup? These statistics brought a twinkle to my eye. A whopping 91% of Americans agree that a clean and neat hairstyle is important, followed closely by 82% who believe light makeup is a definite "do" for a woman's appearance on the job. I try to remind my clients that hair and makeup are not really for you – you can't see you – but everyone else can.

What were the big "don'ts"? Eighty percent believed casual clothes and heavy makeup are not acceptable. Finally, 65% did not think it takes a lot of money to have the kind of clothes, hair, and makeup that make a good impression at work.

Men have instinctively always worn dark suits, and throughout the years, they have branded themselves as successful. When you see a man in a suit, you instantly think "executive," "leader," "owner," "powerful." While women are in varying fields, which may require different dressing strategies, this "Dress For Success" strategy should be applied to dressing for the position you want, not the one you have. Brand yourself. Sara Palin's image consultants dressed her to look presidential (I'm not sure I could have given back all those fabulous suits). Remember the movie "The Devil Wears Prada"? The assistant finally received respect and promotion when she dressed for the position she wanted (or thought she wanted). Branding works.

While your dressing strategy needs to be congruent with your industry and your body type, here are a few general tips that will enhance the way you look.

**Let's Dress To Impress**

*Color*: There is a range of colors that will compliment your skin tone, helping you appear younger, happier, healthier, and even friendlier. While color analysis has come a long way since "Color Me Beautiful" in the 80s, the basic premise is still the same. Certain skin colors look better with cool colors (blue undertones) and others are better with warm colors (yellow undertones). The right colors can literally take 5 to 10 years off! Are you cool or warm? If you are not sure, find a seasoned image professional to help you.

Color choices do affect your professionalism. Here's how you can dress to impress. High contrasting colors, which are a bright and dark combination, are power dressing. Careful with this one, because you could make others feel inferior. Contrast is important, though, because when an onlooker's brain sees this color difference, it literally wakes up. This results in you being remembered, listened to, and taken notice of. Medium contrast, which is light and dark combinations, is the most people-friendly, while being assertive and professional. Low contrast, where all garments are similar colors, sometimes called monochromatic colors, are beautiful and fashionable, but don't make a statement in the business world. No statement, no presence means unforgettable and boring, maybe even invisible. Dark colors convey a message. The darker the color, the more serious and professional you will appear.

*Lines*: Just like color psychology creates favorable or unfavorable impressions, so do lines, textures, shapes, and designs. If you want to dress to impress, use these tried and true techniques that have been around for ages. <u>Never</u> show cleavage at work. Need I say provocative clothing will send a message of lack of self-control and judgment? Look for blouses with darts and vertical button holes. Bosom Buddy is a cute pin that closes low-cut tops and Boob Tubes fill in a low v-necked blouse. <u>Never</u> wear three different patterns in one outfit. Clashing colors or uncoordinated outfits make you appear disorganized. <u>Never</u> wear bright colors where you have a figure challenge. Avoid bringing attention to figure problems. For instance, if you are large or overweight, certain textures will make you look larger. <u>Never</u> wear crisp, stiff, bulky, shiny, or clingy fabrics. Consider the lines and design of the garment. <u>Never</u> wear horizontal; it makes you look shorter and broader.

Know your figure problem areas, i.e., large stomach, broad hips, narrow shoulders. Don't draw attention to a problem area. For instance, large hips look slimmer in an A-line skirt rather than a pencil skirt, and large stomachs look slimmer with a three button jacket rather than a one button jacket. Know your body type and understand your vertical proportions of body to leg length. This determines your best hem, jacket, and coat lengths. Remember, longer skirts look better on long legs. If you are short, wear boots with long skirts. Dressing with dark colors at bottom to light colors at top draws the eyes upward and makes you look slimmer. Vertical lines make you look taller and thinner. Diagonal lines and features are slimming. Horizontal lines and plaids make you look larger. Slimming textures are flat, smooth, matte, and have no surface interest. Patterns should be in direct proportion to your size and bone structure. Patterns with dark backgrounds are more slimming.

Maintain a professional look. Always wear a jacket or third piece. For jacket-only suits, add a great pin or scarf. A blouse and skirt always need a jacket. On casual day, don't be too casual. Wear an outer, opened shirt, light unconstructed jacket, or unbuttoned sweater. Remember, suits cover a multitude of imperfections. Shoulder pads are back, ladies, maybe not quite as dramatic as the 80s, but they're back! I love shoulder pads—who wouldn't want their shoulders to look wider than their hips? Be consistent; don't wear an expensive suit with worn or dirty shoes.

Always try on everything before you buy. The right fit, the right lines, color, texture, and features are key to dressing to impress.

### *Face and Hair Success*

Hair cuts should complement your face shape. Height, weight, neck length, and body type are important factors in creating the correct hairstyle. For instance, if you are 5'1" tall and have broad hips, an extremely short 'boy cut' would not be appropriate, nor would a below the shoulders cut work. Other factors include hair texture and styling abilities. Seek a hair stylist who can design a hairstyle that will work for you and not against you. Avoid trends that are here today and gone tomorrow. A consistent flattering style with slight moderations from time to time establishes a memorable impression and favor.

What about hair color? I'm always asked about grey hair and I always explain that grey hair makes you look older, period. On men it may make them look distinguished, but it still makes them look older. If you are a woman, you will have to examine your goals and how grey hair may affect the message you want to send. If you are close to retirement, grey hair may not matter, but if you want to climb the corporate ladder, receive a promotion with more responsibilities, or need funding for a new business, it may.

Grey hair tends to fare better on Winters, especially when it becomes totally white. The cool, crisp jewel tones the Winter wears look great with 'salt and pepper,' as well. The Summer, who wears cool pastels like baby blue, pinks, and lavender, looks better with soft browns and highlights or ash-blonde hair. Since Springs wear bright, warm colors like yellow, orange, and red, their hair color needs to keep up, as in golden blonde or brunette, red, strawberry blonde, or light auburn. The warm earth tones the Autumn wears look awesome with golden or red-toned brunettes, red, or auburn hair. If you are leery of permanent hair color, semi-permanent will cover grey without changing the rest.

Do you have to wear makeup? Yes, period. Studies have shown that with equally qualified applicants, the one wearing makeup will receive an 8% to 20% higher starting salary. Women who wear makeup are promoted four times more than women who don't. While I can't see your face and be specific, I can give you a few simple pointers that will help you get started or give you a check up from the neck up.

A light professional look consists of well-groomed brows. Remove excess hair between the eyes and under the brow. Fill in sparse areas and cover grey with pencils, brush-on powders, or tint. While eyeliner and eye shadow are not necessary, mascara is. Remember, your brows frame your face, but it is the lashes that frame the eye. If you have few or no lashes, eyeliner is a must.

Unless you have perfectly flawless skin, you will need to wear a makeup base. The perfect makeup base covers imperfections and evens skin tones to promote a healthy-looking facial surface. Men were blessed with thicker skin containing more collagen and elastin than women. That is why their skin surface is not as blotchy and wrinkles much later. While I do have a few male clients who wear foundation because of acne scarring or sun damage, it is rare that men need foundation. Compact and loose powder foundations usually work best on younger, smoother skin. Oil-free liquids work best on oily skin types. Creams or liquid powders are more suitable on dry skin and those with wrinkles and age spots. When applying, cover the entire face (even the eyelids). Use a quilted cotton pad or clean makeup sponge to remove excess around the hair and jaw lines.

Apply a light neutral blush on the apple (that is the plump area of your cheek that is created when you smile). This gives you a healthy, glow or a natural flush of color, not an artificial arch of color out toward your hair line. Brush on and blend edges with a makeup sponge to soften demarcation lines.

Finally, lip color seals the deal. Medium cool (rose, dark pink, soft red) or warm (mocha, rust, or dark peach) colors should remain on your lips all day long. Yes, that means you will have to re-apply after the coffee break, lunch and snack time. If your lipstick bleeds, use a lip liner in the same color family. An invisible lip liner placed just outside the lip line also holds lip color in.

Makeup, hairstyle, and wardrobe work synergistically to produce a positive professional image. Imagine this: a beautiful outfit, great hairstyle, pale and blotchy skin, bushy brows–or worse, no brows–and invisible lips. Just doesn't work, does it? Let me shout it from the desk tops: WEAR MAKEUP!

## HOW YOU ACT

By now you realize you are communicating before you even say a word. Body language is an important aspect of how others see you. Let's make sure we are sending the right message with our body language.

- When you look someone in the eye, you are saying, "I want to know more about you."
- When your eyes are locked onto one part of the face, you are saying, "I am nervous."
- When you look or lean away from a person routinely, you are saying, "I don't like you."
- When you raise an eyebrow, you are saying, "Oh really!"
- When you close your eyes halfway, you are saying, "I am suspicious."
- When you widen your eyes, you are saying, "I am amazed."
- When your jaw drops, you are saying, "I don't believe it."
- When you are constantly looking at the ground, you are saying, "I am unconfident."
- When your head is up, you are saying, "I don't mind people looking at me."
- When your head is down, you are saying, "I don't want people looking at me."
- When your shoulders are open and wide, you are saying, "I would like to meet new people."

These are a few simple examples that will help you be aware of the message of your body language. Be aware that body language does not have the same meaning all over the world. Learn and respect the differences; for instance, in some countries it is impolite to look someone in the eye. The following are a few reliable tips that will speak volumes.

- Stand upright with weight equally distributed on both feet. To look 10 lbs. thinner, turn body slightly so that one foot points toward the twelve o'clock position, the other will point toward the ten o'clock or two o'clock position. Sit up straight with legs crossed at ankles and pulled to the side.
- Walk with your head held high and smile to everyone you meet. Remember, poor posture is associated with a poor self image.
- Be a better than good listener. Listen with your eyes, as well as your ears. Don't interrupt. Nod your head occasionally and stay engaged.
- Introductions made easy: say the name of the most important person first. That includes the boss, a new client, or the eldest relative. Shake hands firmly and maintain eye contact.
- When having a conversation, keep gestures to a minimum because they can be distracting. Display confidence with vocal clarity, good posture, and animated facial expressions. Avoid annoying habits like throat clearing, sniffing, touching your hair, or adjusting your clothes.
- When leaving messages, never ask the person you are calling to call you back. Always get back with them.
- When speaking, imagine you are having a conversation. Slow down, breathe, and speak around 125 to 150 words a minute. This style of conversational speaking will help you appear more pleasant and likeable. For persuasive speaking, kick it up a notch to 200 words per minute.
- The tone of your voice is comprised of various pitches and articulations of words. Speak clearly and in varying rates for emphasis. Never speak in monotone.

Finally, did you know your mood was controlled by your face? I often hear preachers say to their congregation, "Is everyone blessed and happy?" The congregation will nod their heads and he replies, "Well, you need to tell your face about it." Physiognomy is the science of facial features and their effect on the brain. The way the mind works is that it notices the patterns in your facial features and reflects your actual mood accordingly. Reverend Amy Hayes Dockery once preached, "You can't pray your way into alignment; you must act your way into alignment." Remember your mother saying that she did not like the way you were acting and others saying you need to get your act together? We are all acting out this life in front of a very observant audience. Now that you know that actions do speak louder than words, try to win an Oscar for your performance.

## HOW YOU THINK

According to Theresa Merchant, author of *The Importance of Image,* "Appearances are only part of it; without anything to give power to your appearance, regardless how fine or expensive an outfit may be, your true image may still be weak." Someone once said that who you are speaks so loudly, I can't hear what you are saying.

How you think about yourself can truly define you and dominate your image. It is the essence of you and can dictate what you wear, how you stand, what you say, what your mood is, and the tone of your voice. The dictionary says that 'self image' is the idea, conception or mental image one has of oneself.

Imagine the perfect makeover: great hairstyle, perfect makeup, and figure-flattering clothes in the correct color palette. You look fabulous (or should I say gorgeous), but you don't feel fabulous. Old fears and thoughts paralyze you. No smiles, no eye contact, negative body language, disgruntled attitude, and silence spell defeat. Theresa is right, no matter how good you look, that belief and confidence in yourself (a positive self image) that completes your total image must be there in order to spell success.

I asked my friend Cheryl Grey, a licensed counselor, about how the self image is formed. She said that your self-image is based on the relationship you have with yourself, and that relationship is based on what you believe about yourself, and what you believe about yourself is based on thoughts. According to Cheryl's research, thoughts are formed from two sources. *Source one* is what others have said about you that you have come into agreement with. These are words you have accepted as fact and operate upon. This agreement influences what you do and how much effort you put into it. *Source two* is your interpretation of the events and circumstances in your life.

I just heard Dr. Carolyn Leaf speak again. She is a neuro-scientist who has done extensive research on the brain and, as always, my hand couldn't write the notes fast enough. Research now reveals that thoughts make neuro-pathways in the brain that look somewhat like trees. The more you think about it, the more branches and leaves you grow on those trees. Proper thoughts look like healthy trees and toxic thoughts look like Charlie Browns' Christmas tree. Science now has proven that we were created to love and not hate, to think good and positive thoughts. When we do, the correct chemicals are produced by the hypothalamus and we are healthy and happy. When you think toxic thoughts that are not natural for you, then cortisol and other unhealthy chemicals are formed and stress and anxiety begin an unhealthy route to sickness and disease. Dr. Leaf says, "A massive body of research collectively shows that up to 80% of physical, emotional and mental health issues today could be a direct result of our thought lives."

Of course, I am just summarizing a lifetime of research and studies that is just fascinating to me. It gives new meaning to the song "Don't worry, be happy," doesn't it? What was also interesting was the fact that you can change those unhealthy trees in your brain. In her book Who Switched Off My Brain, she explains toxic thoughts and steps to change them. Isn't it interesting that the Word tells us to be "born again" and "renew our minds"?

As you go through life, things happen. People and circumstances put thoughts into your mind. Unfortunately you may not have been blessed with a perfect life. Who has? The good news is that the negative, toxic thoughts can be overcome. You can re-brainwash (not sure that is a real word) yourself. The Bible calls it "washing of the water of the word." Mike Murdock, an inspirational speaker, says if you change your mind, you can change what you do. Identify those toxic thoughts that are damaging your self-image and maybe even your health. Replace those Charlie Brown Christmas trees with beautiful, healthy trees, full of leaves and branches that make you feel good about yourself and your future. Examine your perception of the circumstances of your life. Forgive the past you regret and the people who have hurt you, so you can move forward. You are not the only one who has made a bad choice or two and yes, there are really mean people out there (sometimes they are even relatives) who are bent on the destruction of others. Forgiveness doesn't mean that it is OK and it didn't hurt, it just means you have learned from it, you are letting go of it, and you are moving forward, free of its control.

Prayer and meditation are great tools for reconstructing or improving your self-image. Ask God for wisdom so you can understand how special and unique you are. Meditation means muttering to oneself. What are you muttering? Yes, self-talk is OK as long as it reinforces your worth. Your goal is to build your self-image (how you think), which actually enhances your performance (how you act) and improves how you look. That is the total package: your total image that others see.

## CONCLUSION

I am reminded of the Bible story of David being chosen to be the future King. God told the prophet Samuel to go find Jesse; that one of his sons was to become king. Jesse brought his seven sons before the prophet one by one but none of them were right. Jesse paraded his most comely and best; surely one of these was the one. "Are here all thy children?" the prophet asked. Jesse explained that there was the youngest son tending sheep. Samuel said to fetch him. David was "ruddy" and without a beautiful countenance and not goodly to look upon. The Lord told Samuel to arise and anoint him, for "this is he" (1 Samuel 16:5-12).

The Lord had told Samuel, "Look not on his countenance or on the height of his stature; because I have refused him (talking about the other sons of Jesse), for the Lord seeth not as a man seeth; for man looketh on the outward appearance but the Lord looketh on the heart." It's soooo good to know that God loves you no matter what your appearance is, but He did give us a giant clue as to how man is going to judge you. That's just the way it is.

Now you see why *image matters*. How you look, how you act and how you think produce a powerful image that others examine, make deductions from, and choose favorably or unfavorably. Your total image can give you favor to open doors and make lasting impressions. Remember, you are always *networking*, so always dress, act, and think in such a way that will give others a favorable experience of you.

# NUGGET #4 continued

## Your Image – Business & Personal

### Introduction by Debra Pope

Image is one of the most important components of your *networking*. We must give attention to detail in the way we present ourselves.

Now, I'd like to introduce you to another lady who devotes her time and life promoting the positive image of others. I've had the opportunity to get to know her through *networking* as well, and I am in awe of her wisdom and expertise in helping others with their image. She is a caring and successful business woman and a true entrepreneur: Christi Harris.

For over 30 years, Christi's passion for turning basic beauty into greater beauty has resonated with literally thousands of loyal followers. It is from this experiential and educational background that Christi again and again saw women's frustrations with skin and hair care products, as well as cosmetics.

With the myriad options on the market, from department stores to drug stores, she witnessed too many women purchasing promises that did not deliver. She then set out to make a difference, developing skin and hair treatments based on the physiology of our bodies, and cosmetics that created a flawless, yet natural finish. And the most important concept of all was offering the education women craved, and heretofore had been denied, to become their own best beauty expert.

A renowned beauty expert, Christi is regularly published in national magazines and beauty blogs around the world. She can be seen frequently on network talk shows and is a regular guest on "Great Day Houston" and "Good Morning Texas."

The Christi Harris product line is available through her flagship Christi Harris Beaute' Playgrounds in Dallas and Houston, Texas, as well as department stores, salons, electronic retailers such as ShopNBC, direct response infomercials and online.

She is sought for her experience, wisdom and advice in all things beauty, including remedying frustrations, speaking truths and dispelling myths. Christi has developed hundreds of exquisite products in skin, hair and body treatments and professional makeup. She continues to create user-friendly, affordable products and tools, teaching techniques that simply deliver. She is revolutionizing the archaic way brows have been shaped for centuries with her latest creation, The Christi Harris Precision Brow Planing System. Christi's philosophy, "See it. Learn it. Do it," empowers teens and women of all ages and lifestyles to appreciate their individual beauty and perfect their preferred look, maximizing both confidence and charisma! And as she often says, *"There is no such thing as an unattractive woman ... simply an untrained one."*

**Christi Harris**
**The Beaute Playgounds**
**ChristiHarris@ChristiHarris.com**
**972 866-8500**

## Your Image – Business and Personal

### By Christi Harris

The rural west Texas town of my childhood was delightfully long on charm and hospitality, but abysmally short on any access to or even suggestion of fashion and beauty. Each month I'd wait impatiently for my *Seventeen* magazine to arrive in our mailbox. Not only was it the only magazine my mother allowed me to read, it was also the sole related fashion-resource this savvy young girl had to reference. My girlfriends and I would peruse the pages, yearning to look like the gorgeous models—the clothes, hairstyles and makeup—but not one of us knew how to mimic their looks. There were no department stores or malls, no one to educate us, and our only source for cosmetics was limited to the town drugstore. We spent hours playing with our makeup, trying different colors and techniques, but truly had no idea what we were doing. Was it too much? Not enough? The right color? If by some chance we received a compliment, then that was a clue that maybe we had actually accomplished something from the hours spent in front of the mirror, though our quest continued.

As I got older, I enjoyed watching beauty pageants and from those experiences began to understand how critical one's image is to success. The contestants walked gracefully and held their heads high. I wanted that but did not know how to pull it off and make it work for me. I'd look in the mirror, not disliking what I saw necessarily, but knowing I could improve—look better and more beautiful—with the right knowledge and products. By this time, I had accumulated drawers-full of random cosmetics that only left me frustrated and disappointed.

When I left home for college, I was introduced to department stores. I'd died and gone to makeup heaven! Until I realized that, though the selection was improved, there was little offered in the way of education…no one was teaching how to apply "pretty" makeup. Thus I continued collecting makeup and skin care that didn't deliver.

My passion for knowledge fueled my search for someone, *anyone*, who could mentor me.

Skip ahead—following a year at Abilene Christian University, I relocated to Dallas, Texas to pursue my dream. As a new student at Wade's Fashion Merchandising College, Ms. Wade encouraged me to consider modeling. To facilitate my aspirations, she referred me to the one of the best stylists in town for a makeover. I was a sponge for the stylist's techniques and tips. Finally I'd found a resource for the information I'd been craving!

That initial makeover was my catapult not only to modeling, but ultimately to my professional success. I learned more of fashion and image, gaining poise and a better understanding of the art of communication and body language. I absorbed every snippet I could about cosmetics, skincare, hair, and virtually all things beauty, until the day came when I was bursting with knowledge and I knew it was my calling to share it with anyone who would listen. God delivered that opportunity to me when, at 19, I joined the educators at John Robert Powers Modeling Schools, writing curriculum and teaching others self-improvement. At 21, my research was demonstrated and verifiable, but I could not find products that coincided with what I knew to be truth. My cosmetics line was launched from that need to provide my students products that were compatible with the knowledge I had and the curriculum I was authoring. It was my mission to save them the exasperating frustration I'd felt in my earlier years.

My passion ultimately became my life-long career as I built a foundation based upon five basic principles. In sharing these principles, it must also be said that not only will they be helpful in your profession, they also will serve you well in your daily life.

1. Believe your inner voice when she speaks to you. Listen and know what you love to do, then do your own research, not taking that of others as truth until you've proven it yourself. If you simply follow others, you will become them and lose what makes you uniquely you.

2. Search for common unmet needs and continuing frustrations of others within your industry and work to meet those needs and squelch those frustrations. Not only will you be amazingly successful, you will be a hero to many!
3. Know your facts and resources and be ready and willing to prove them. If you are unsure about the information you are relaying, how can the listener possibly be sure? Do not be afraid to state what makes you and your business, product or service superior to the competition, keeping in mind that degrading or disparaging your competitors will never—ever—serve anyone …most especially you.
4. Build strong relationships with your customers and clients. This may seem elementary but it remains a mystery to many—even in today's challenging and increasingly competitive environment, great service is not a given. That can be experienced in any industry in any city. If you take these relationships seriously, your customers and clients will, as well, and it will manifest in mutual loyalty.
5. Do not lie. Do not burn bridges. When you believe in yourself and the work you do, there is no need to stretch the truth, oversell or take advantage of another.

**Your Image. Your Success.**

My passion, of course, is self-improvement and the beauty business. I sincerely believe that genuine beauty comes from within. I get it. But let me share, it is so much easier to feel better from the inside when you know you look good on the outside!

Now let's get serious. Oh, I mean it…really serious. Look in the mirror. What would you like to see appear differently? We *all* have areas we'd like to improve. In this exercise, neither be overly critical nor shy. Remember, we are not talking about perfection. Past the age of accountability, "perfect" is a fantasy that only Photoshop can create, so let's release that expectation right here, right now.

What I witness daily is not an "I hate everything" attitude; rather, the desire for a tweak here and a tweak there. Moreover, the most often requested service at our Beaute' Playgrounds is simply an "update." Nothing crazy, nothing that makes you look like someone else, but a little boost to break us out of our boredom and keep up with current trends and freshen our look. Listen when I tell you I have worked with literally thousands of women since the 18th century. LOL. Not quite that long, but long enough to know that a makeover is the fastest, easiest, safest and least expensive avenue to a new sense of self. Remember my experience at 19. I was desperate to look the part, fit in, be a popular cheerleader, maybe one day even have a boyfriend. My makeover helped me understand that it was neither essential nor even appropriate for me to look like all the others, but to look my best…*my very own personal best.* As a bonus, it even helped me with my weight struggles because I was so motivated from the immediate gratification of the makeover!

Begin at the beginning. From head to toe makes sense. Start with your face…Invest in the highest quality (within your means), proven skin care and makeup products. I said "highest quality," not "highest price," because price does not always denote quality when it comes to beauty products.

Build a collection of professional makeup brushes. You cannot get professional results without professional makeup brushes. Seek information and education. Learn to do your own facials and be your own makeup artist, giving you the confidence to apply makeup that lasts all day or all night, be it for the office, a night out on the town or a special occasion.

And for the love of all things beautiful, get a handle on your brows. The brows frame the most expressive feature on your face. A well-shaped, shaded brow is brilliant. A bad brow—from bushy and unkempt to skinny and skimpy—is a disaster sticking right out from the middle of your face. And while I am up here on my brow soap box, for Heaven's sake do not ever, ever tweeze, wax or thread your brows, or you could wake up one day with *no* brows at all. It's the truth. Brow planing is a safer, more precise technique for achieving the perfect brow.

Then move to your hair…I will say this again for emphasis—move to your hair. Getting a great hairstyle suited to your hair type, face shape and lifestyle will make as much of an impact as makeup. And do not ignore your hair color, either. The right hair color can stop traffic. The wrong hair color is a train wreck. Keep it fresh. If you are sporting the same hairstyle you had two years ago (or God forbid, five or even ten years ago), it's time to shake things up. Take a look around. Television, movies and magazines are all great resources for the latest looks. And truthfully, YouTube videos and professional beauty bloggers can be incredibly helpful! I constantly update my website with educational postings and "How To" videos on all things beauty. Try looks, styles and techniques that make sense. Be realistic. Solicit the help of a professional whenever possible, either virtually or face-to-face. Here's how…

Get started on your quest for a great makeover by calling a nearby major department store and speaking to their fashion director or store manager. Most are happy to refer you to the modeling agency they use for special events. Call the agency and ask for a referral to a professional makeup artist and hairstylist who can design a fabulous new look for you. This may cost $150 to $350 for a makeover, depending on your market, but understand it will save money and potentially heartache in the long run. Be open-minded for change at your appointment because you are likely to get just that with professionals. It's what they are there for and what they do. Draw on their expertise. Be sure the artists teach you how to recreate your look at home. I suggest taking your own hair and makeup brushes as well as your primary makeup collection so they may see what you are comfortable working with.

Fashion and style follows face and hair. Begin with a fashion stylist, a professional who can pull everything together for you. Google "Fashion Stylist (city)" in your area. Ask their specialty (casual, corporate, formal) and do find out as much as you can about their professional background. They will be happy to share that information. Peruse their websites if available. Again, a reputable modeling agency can be a great resource for a fashion stylist. Keep in mind, department stores, personal shoppers, wardrobe consultants or image consultants typically sell clothes. A fashion stylist works with you to develop the image you want to portray on a budget you can live within, often saving you hundreds of dollars on clothes that may not be the best additions to your closet. Most will begin with what you already own, adding a few necessary pieces seasonally, keeping you hip to the latest styles and trends.

Splurging on fabulous, crazy-expensive pieces can make for a fun day of shopping, but being fashionable does *not* have to cost a fortune. Great higher-end labels offered at discounted prices can be found at Neiman Marcus Last Call and Nordstrom Rack. Target, Zara, TJ Maxx, and other discounters offer terrific options, as well.

Carrying a few extra libbys? Many of us, myself included, struggle with our weight from time to time. I am currently learning as much as possible about alkaline foods. Science suggests we cannot gain weight on alkaline foods! How fantastic is that? I'm not a physician and cannot advise you specifically as to an appropriate weight management program. What works for me may not work for you. However, I encourage you to take action against the damaging effects of excess weight. This is not only a matter of aesthetics, but so many health issues can manifest from being overweight. Eat sensibly, work out or enjoy some type of exercise and stay strong!

You deserve it all, but you must believe it and know that you can have it all. The right professionals can help you get there. Seek their expertise now so that you don't wake up someday and say, "I wish I'd known these things years ago." Working with professionals can not only help you look great and manage your wardrobe, but may mean the difference in landing that client, promotion or new job you've worked so hard for. If your credentials and reputation are sound, yet your results aren't showing as you feel they should, take inventory of your image. Image can be the determining factor in closing the deal. As is said so often, you only have one chance to make a first impression. Use it wisely. Make a commitment to yourself, your present and your future. Dare to dream and when you do, dream big! My career vision began with the colorful pages of my Seventeen magazine…and now my products are often featured in that same publication, among others. Did today's reality seem even remotely possible to me as a young west Texas girl? No. But with my dream of working in fashion and self-improvement came the determination to work as hard as I must to share my passion and knowledge with other women, forever alleviating their beauty frustrations. Do what you love. Love what you do. The results will astound you!

Lastly, let me share that regardless of our outward appearance—as important as it is to our success—we cannot be our best, most successful selves if our hearts and minds are not in the right place. Take good care of both your physical and spiritual self. Count your blessings. Stand in gratitude. Walk in beauty and light, and live in peace. You are beautiful!

Hugs,
Christi Harris

# NUGGET #5

## Your Business Card - Your Mini Billboard

### By Debra Pope

Even with the advances in technology, a business card is as important now as ever before. The design of business your card is critical. You only get one chance to make a first impression, and your card is as much a part of that first impression as your personal appearance.

Your business logo is also critical. You may need to use the skills of a graphic artist to create your logo, even if you have a sketch, drawing or an idea of what it should look like. This is one of the most critical aspects of creating and establishing "your brand."

Your business card must be designed to attract clients, like a flower attracts a bee. Your business card should be consistent in color, type style and font and carry your logo, to achieve the maximum impact when you give them out in person at a *networking* event, and for all marketing materials, sales and advertising use. As you establish your company and yourself in business, people you meet will begin to remember you by your logo, business card design and advertising campaigns if they are kept consistent in look and design.

Make sure the back of the card is left blank or has an area for notes so that you can write information for the prospective client when you meet them or for the referral or lead you want to give.

Your business card should have as much information about you and your company as possible. You want to include your logo, company name, physical or mailing address, phone number, e-mail address, slogan or tag line. You want to give as much information on the card as possible to make sure the prospective client or person you have referred can follow up with you easily without having to dig for your contact information.

The size of the font for the card should be large enough to be easily read. Many times I've encountered business cards with the font and typestyle so microscopic that they are nearly impossible to read without a magnifying glass.

Be sure to include your e-mail address on your business cards. While omitting your e-mail address might help avoid spam, if a prospective client or referral needs to contact you, I recommend having your business e-mail address on the card.

Too much information is as bad as not enough. Make sure your business card includes your contact information so clients can easily find you when your products or services are needed, and you won't get passed over for another business that is more easily located.

There are many styles of business cards. Most business cards are designed in the landscape orientation. A smaller percentage of them are designed in the portrait orientation.

I don't recommend you design your business cards in an oversize or odd shape. The oddly shaped or odd-sized business cards do "stick out" in a group of cards that your fellow *networking* attendees have received, but they are difficult to keep for follow-up or storage if they are larger or an odd size and shape.

If you have more information about your product than you can get on a single business card, a double fold card is appropriate.

Even though a double fold card is more expensive to print than a single card, you may find that it takes the place of flyers, which may cut down on your marketing costs in the long run.

Make sure you never, ever leave your home or office without your business cards. Never attend a *networking* event without cards. It amazes me how many people will attend an event, and don't bring their business cards!

Even if you are going jogging, out to dinner, to a family reunion or on a quick trip to the grocery store; don't forget your business cards. If your day includes a workout at the gym, or an outing to the beach, be sure to bring your business cards. Have your cards in your pocket, sock or in your car. If you don't bring them, I promise, you will need them.

Veteran networkers call this being "loaded." Make sure you have your "load" of business cards in case you need them.

The business card, while small in size, plays a big part in your success. It has an amazing impact on how you appear to prospective clients you meet or the business relationships you make as a result of giving out your card at a *networking* event.

If well designed, your business card will continue to bring you business, referrals and goodwill long after the *networking* event you attended is past.

My personal preference is to keep business cards I have received. By simply making a visual scan through the business cards in my collection, I will remember the person, their business, the service or product they had to offer and whether they were a "Giving first, sharing always" type of person.

# NUGGET #6

## Business Card Management

### By Debra Pope

I'm amazed that small things can be so important! A tiny key opens the door to a car, home or huge building. Something as tiny as a business card is so valuable. Business cards play such an important role in your *networking*. Keeping a supply of your own cards and receiving them at events can cause a challenge unless you have a plan.

When preparing to attend a *networking* event, be sure you have plenty of business cards with you.

I recommend you have a business card holder to keep your own personal cards and a card holder to put the cards you receive at the event or even throughout your work day. There are hundreds of types of business card holders for women and men. They come in masculine or feminine styles and colors. A variety of business card holders are available at gift shops, office supply stores or luggage stores.

The most economical, simple method is to use two small clear sandwich snack packs. Put your own cards in one, and have one to place the cards you receive while at an event. You may want to label the sandwich packs with file folder labels to identify the location and date of the *networking* event where you received the cards until you process them into your database.

You can also use the simple system of placing your cards in your right pocket and the cards you receive in your left pocket.

When you return to your office after attending a *networking* event, you may wonder what to do with the cards you've received. If you throw them into a box or file, there is no benefit to you or the people you've received the cards from. You need a plan to manage the cards you receive.

There are a variety of ways to organize the cards you've received. One method is to put them in three-ring binders in clear plastic "sleeves." You can use dividers to organize the cards you have received alphabetically, by the event, city, type of business or many other categories.

After you have determined the filing system for the cards you've received, how do you use the information on the cards? There are a variety of database systems available. Microsoft Outlook is the most popular for contact management, integrating a calendar system, e-mail and follow up.

Card Scan is a system to feed business cards through, which records the name, company and information from the cards. Cards are fed through the card scanner one at a time. After the scan is complete from each card, the information is displayed on your computer screen. You will need to verify the information and then save the contact information. This method works if the card is the traditional size in landscape orientation. If the card you've received is a two-fold or other odd size, you will need to manually enter the contact information.

Your choice may be to dispose of the cards after you have entered them in to your database. My preference is to keep the business cards I receive in clear, plastic business card holders that fit in three-ring binders. If I feel a good connection with the person I've just met, I ask them for two or three cards. Then, when I'm asked for a referral, I go through my three-ring binders to get the business card of the person I'm referring.

When reviewing the cards I receive, seeing the person's business card with logo, color and design jogs my memory about them. It helps to paint a picture in my mind, allowing me to better remember the person and the business they own or represent.

Whatever method you choose, whether to dispose of or keep the business cards you collect, make good use of the information on the small "gold nugget" of information you have "mined" that is in your possession.

# NUGGET #7

## Networking Etiquette

Lenda Fidelman has lived and learned etiquette through her military service and college career. Lenda understands that in *networking*, as in life, courtesy and respect for others raises the bar and standard to a higher level. She joined the US Army National Guard as a young woman and throughout her six-year commitment in the US Army, she served in many capacities, assisting high ranking officers both domestically and internationally. She graduated from Dallas Baptist University in Dallas, TX with a Bachelor' of Business Studies and is continuing there to achieve her Masters of Business Administration. She's married to A. J. Fidelman and is the mother of a young son, Lance.

**Lenda Fidelman**
**Studio Fidelity**
LendaLee@email.com

# Networking Etiquette

### By Lenda Lee Fidelman

Presenting your best – Networking Etiquette is all about thinking of others first and showing your best side. When networking, you will be meeting many new professionals and it is very important, professionally, to always show your best side and your care and concern for others by using the 3 P's:

- **Polished**
- **Polite**
- **Punctual**

If you work on your 3 P's you will always be perceived as having good *networking* etiquette and you will be more successful in your *networking*. Working on your 3 P's will make you appear approachable, professional, and memorable.

**Polished** - In order to present your best side, you must first look the part; you need to be polished looking. I like to think of it as putting together a puzzle. Each piece needs to fit just right. I start with my own personal appearance and then start to move outward by working on the items that surround me. When I'm *networking* there are two things that I always notice about a person's appearance: their teeth and their hands, because we always smile at each other and shake hands when we first meet. You don't have to have major dental work done to have a nice smile; simply having your teeth whitened will make a huge difference. I know some men feel intimidated about the idea of having their nails worked on, but you don't have to do a professional manicure–just put some lotion on your hands and buff your nails.

Next, I ensure that my hair has been professionally cut and styled. I recommend going to a professional stylist or cosmetologist and asking them to do an assessment of your needs. It will help greatly to have the opinion of an expert when it comes to your hair. Try to stay away from flashy colors or edgy cuts because this can actually distract from your business. Instead, try to stick with a traditional look.

Then, I make sure I have a professional outfit that isn't revealing or tight. It doesn't matter if you're a woman or a man, if your clothes don't fit you won't look professional. I have seen both men and women look ridiculous with super low cut tops in a professional setting. A man showing his hairy chest or a woman showing off a large bust is not attractive in a professional *networking* event. I recommend shopping at a reputable department store like Nordstrom's, where a professional personal shopper can help you to pick out the right outfit for your work environment and have it tailored to fit your body type. Another plus of using a personal shopper is you will be able to tell the shopper what price range you feel comfortable staying in.

Once your personal appearance has been taken care of, it is time to move to your surroundings. Keeping your promotional items together will also enhance your polished image. Ensure that you have all of your business cards, flyers, signage, and other promotional items stored neatly, ready for transportation, and easy to hand out. Keep extra rubber bands and paper clips on hand when attending *networking* events, because you will be meeting other professionals who will be giving you their information. You don't want to throw it in a pile and shove it under the seat you're sitting in. It can be a very positive thing for you to accept promotional items from others and then neatly bind them with a clip and put them in your briefcase or hold them during the meeting to take notes about that person's business, so you can follow up with them later. This goes hand in hand with politeness.

**Polite** - It can mean the difference between having a successful *networking* experience or not. If you aren't perceived as being polite, you won't be approachable. Many people don't even realize when they are being rude or unapproachable. To be polite, you must be aware of yourself and those around you. Taking a self-inventory is the best way to begin. Ask yourself a few questions before entering the *networking* event: "Am I in a good mood today? Have I had a good start to the day? Do I feel like meeting new people and speaking enthusiastically about my business?" If you don't feel like you are in a good mood or things aren't going your way, I suggest you do a quick pick-me-up exercise. Listen to a song that makes you happy, think of a funny joke, and tell yourself that you are about to meet new exciting people who are going to help you excel in your business. If you wake up in the morning with a smile on your face, you are going to go far in this world. People who pretend to be happy when they don't completely feel like it actually end up happier than those who don't.

Next, you need to move to the outside and be aware of those around you. Think before you speak and if you think it could offend someone, don't say it. Telling a joke at a *networking* event can be a quick way to get noticed, but no joke is worth hurting your fellow networkers, so make sure that it is clean and can't be taken out of context.

Once you have a good self-inventory and you have become aware of those around you it's time for you to start *networking*. A good way to meet new people is to smile at them. This gets you noticed and makes the other networkers want to approach you. Hold out your hand to shake theirs, smile at them, and say "It's nice to meet you!" This has made you approachable; now you should ask them about their business.

One of Debra Pope's *Networking* Nuggets is, "It's not about me, it's about we!" Ask them about their business by saying, "What line of work are you in?" This has now shown that you are interested in them, and it will in turn cause them to ask you about your business, giving you the opportunity to give them your thirty-second commercial and your promotional materials.

Finally, you will want to take any of the promotional information that they have to give you, put it neatly in your briefcase and, most importantly, say, "Thank you for the information. It has been great to meet you. I will call you to follow up on our conversation." With that being said, you have been approachable, friendly, and memorable, and you have left the door open to do your follow-up call and be able to do business together. Ensure that at the end of the *networking* event you make it a point to thank the host for having you and thank the speaker for the useful information. This leads me to being punctual.

**Punctual** - While listed as the final step, it really should be in your mind from the beginning. You want to not only strive to arrive at events on time but also complete your follow-up in a timely manner. If you tell the people you have met that you will e-mail or call them, do it the same day as the event or no later than following day, while you and your business are fresh in their minds. This is polite and lets them know that you are a person of your word.

Keep a calendar at all times to remember what you have scheduled. This is the number one thing you must do. Try to keep an annual calendar for important dates like birthdays, anniversaries, holidays, vacations, and deadlines for projects. Then, keep a calendar that is weekly and more detailed, with activities that might not be on a regular basis, like *networking* events, follow up calls, or business meetings. I enjoy and recommend using Microsoft Outlook because I can print the calendar to carry it with me, make changes easily, and it can break down your calendar to be annual, monthly, weekly, and daily. There are multiple other things you can do with Outlook that can be very beneficial, and there are several services that are similar. Whatever you decide to use, the point is to try to keep it digitally so you can update it and access it easily or print it to carry with you if you're like me.

Always schedule enough time to be prepared on the day prior to any *networking* event or appointment. You should be looking over your calendar at the beginning of every week to ensure you don't have a last minute panic attack due to a meeting that you forgot about or a dreaded double booking. Everyone has done it at least once, so don't feel awful if you accidentally double book someone; just ensure that you apologize and reschedule as soon as possible.

Chances are they have had it happen to them and hearing your honesty will help smooth things out.

When I arrive at a *networking* event I like to get there early: thirty minutes prior to the start time should give you plenty of time to get signed in, find a good seat, and give you a chance to do a little *networking* before the beginning of the event. If you schedule to arrive at a *networking* event early, you will almost never be late and you can avoid a major amount of stress, from trying to find a parking spot in a full lot to being embarrassed by coming in after the speaker has started. The added bonus of getting to network ahead of time can be huge because you will get more one on one time with the people you came to talk to.

In closing I want to highlight the most important things that you should be doing to ensure you have good networking etiquette:

**Polished**
- Ensure your appearance is put together and professional.
- Have your promotional materials organized and easily accessible.
- Keep rubber bands or paper clips on hand to organize the material you are given.

**Polite**
- Present yourself as having a good positive attitude.
- Smile.
- Shake everyone's hand that you meet and make sure they know you how happy you are to have met them.
- Say thank you to everyone you meet, including the host and speaker.

**Punctual**
- Keep a calendar of events to ensure you are on time and not double booked.
- Arrive thirty minutes early to a *networking* event.
- Follow up with the people you meet the same day or no later than the following day.

# NUGGET #8

## Your Elevator Speech and Tag Line

### Introduction By Debra Pope

You may not be familiar with the term "Elevator Speech." If not, let me explain with this example: You've tried for months to get an appointment with the CEO of a company that you know could use your services. You can never get past the "Gatekeeper" and you've just left the receptionist with yet another turn-down, another "no" to the request for an appointment with the CEO or the "decision maker." You leave the office and get on the elevator to leave. Lo and behold! The CEO you've been trying to meet is with you on the elevator! You have only a few seconds to tell him about you and your services. You must be <u>prepared</u>. We all wish we could be so lucky as to meet that much sought out CEO in the elevator, and if we do, we need to be ready!

The most common use of an "Elevator Speech" is at a *networking* event. At most formal *networking* events, your presentation is actually timed to make sure that every attendee has the same amount of time allotted to make their presentation.

The more common lengths of time allotted at most *networking* events are 30 seconds, 60 seconds, or possibly two minutes.

I recommend you write or type your commercial to accommodate the 30 second time frame, 60 seconds and two minutes. Then practice makes perfect, and it's best to be in front of your mirror. This will help take away some of the panic by giving you practice before you're in front of a group.

Start with writing your 30 second commercial. It may seem awkward or "silly" at first, but after you practice reading your commercial out loud, then memorizing it for presentation, it gets easier. It's important to speak clearly, enunciate and speak loudly. Make sure you begin and end with your name, your company and your position at your company. Time your commercial to make sure it fits in to the allotted time of 30 seconds. If you have access to a recorder, record your 30 second commercial and listen to it. Does it sound enthusiastic? Are you speaking clearly? Are you speaking loudly enough to be heard by all in the room? If you have a video recorder with a tripod, record yourself doing the commercial. Remember your body language, stance, presence, tone, and volume are important as what you are saying. Have you heard the line: "**It's not just what you say, it's how you say it**"?

It's important to make eye contact, stand up straight, gesture if appropriate and have a "prop" if appropriate during your commercial.

**Creating Your "Tag Line" or "Hook"**: Human beings have a very short attention span, so it is important to have a "Tag Line" or a "Hook" when you are doing your commercial at a Networking event. When I was in the travel industry, my tag line was "**I get to tell you where to go.**" Later in my career, when I owned fitness centers, my tag line became: "**I used to tell you where to go; now I tell you how to stick around**"!

Create a tag line that pertains to you, your business or your name that is catchy, memorable or humorous. The goal is to be unique and to get your listeners' attention so they will remember you and your business.

Once you've mastered your 30 second commercial, write your 60 second commercial. As with the 30 second commercial, begin and end with your name, your company name and your position with your company. You'll have a bit more time to teach your *networking* partners about you, your mission, and the service or products you provide.

After you've attended the same *networking* event many times and have gotten your *networking* partners educated about you and your company, you may want to change it up a bit.

If you can come up with a humorous twist to your commercial, people will enjoy your presentation and look forward to hearing your commercial. I've heard people who sing their commercial, recite a poem about their business, dress like a cheerleader complete with pom-poms, and wear other odd costumes. The AFLAC agents bring a duck that quacks at the end of their commercials, the plumber brings a miniature toilet complete with flushing sound effects, the web site repair people come with a lab coat and stethoscope saying they'll fix your sick computer and other catchy get-ups and phrases. Do whatever it takes, as long as it's in good taste, to get your fellow *networking* partners to remember you when the time comes and they need your service or will refer you to someone who does.

As an example, below is my **30 Second Commercial and Tag Line**:

*I'm Debra Pope with eWomenNetwork, the #1 organization for promoting and connecting professional women worldwide. We provide opportunities for women to meet, connect, build relationships and do business.*

*My business is connecting you and your business!*
*I'm Debra Pope with eWomenNetwork, your business connector!*

One of the most unique and effective elevator speeches and tag lines that I've ever heard is from a friend of mine, Brian Padden.

Brian has over 25 years experience in data center operations management and telecommunications consulting for multiple Fortune 1000, 100 and 50 companies, including management and director positions at Xerox, EDS, Verizon and telecom-related consulting companies. Brian has a Bachelor of Science in Business and Economics from Tampa University and earned his MBA in Telecommunications Management at the University of Dallas-Graduate School of Management.

**Brian Padden, President/CEO**
**HxP and Associates, Inc. Co-Founder**
**www.hxpassociates.com**

**Brian's 30-Second Commercial and Tag Line**:

> "As a non-biased telecom consultant representing all telecom carriers and all telephone system manufacturers, I coordinate the telecom selection and installation requirements for first-time businesses. When a client is already in business, I help them reduce their monthly recurring telecom expenses. And if the business or organization is growing or moving, I provide carrier and telephone system choices. **And best of all, I don't charge my clients. . . .. so that makes me a free telecom consultant, and not a <u>phony</u>!** "

At the end of Brian's elevator speed and tag line, he throws a ringing cell phone at an unsuspecting fellow networker, which always gets a rise out of the group. Everyone at the Networking event laughs when Brian gives his commercial and tag line. But even more importantly, they remember him forever!

Another great 30 second commercial is the one presented by Dr. Virginia Wells, PhD:

> *Good Morning! I'm Dr. V, The Business Doctor. I help business leaders focus, prioritize, and take action in their business so they can grow them faster, better, and more profitably. Imagine how your business would look, feel, and be, if you had your own personal navigator to keep you on your planned course during all the storms. Talk to me today so I can help you have the best year ever. I am Dr. V., the cure for what ails your business.*

Be sure to write out your 30 and 60 second commercials.

Following is a work sheet for you to use for you write your 60 second commercial:

## 60 Second Introduction Outline

Hi, my name is _____

The name of my company is _____

I/we provide/offer_____

_____

The type of client/customer/job that I'm looking for in the next 30 days _____

_____

_____

What I'm looking to purchase in the next 30-60 days is _____

_____

_____

My Name is _____

My Company is_____

# NUGGET #9

## *Networking* for Career Search Or Career Advancement

### By Debra Pope

We've all heard "It's not what you know, but who you know" when it comes to finding your dream job or career.

Throughout the years I've been asked by friends or acquaintances for advice and referrals on what to do during their job search. My advice to them is to begin with the design of an intriguing, factual, and attractive resume.

 The next step is careful attention to the image you want to portray. In other words, dress for success. Wear your best to look the part for the position you'd like to have.

The next step is to be specific in knowing what position you want and have 30 second and 60 second commercials stating who you are and what strong points you possess.

The next step is to go to *networking* events where the potential employers will be. Not only does *networking* warm up a cold call in sales, but Networking warms up a cold interview.

When on sales calls visiting a business, more times than not, I've been invited in to the office of the CEO because I met him or her at a *networking* event.

Recently at a women's career seminar, I sat at lunch with several of the participants who were there for assistance in their job search. In conversation, the topic led to what websites were available on line to post your résumé. Everyone at my table confessed that while they had listed their resumes on all the major sites, they had not gotten one call for an interview.

My advice was for them to do their research to find the *networking* events in our region where the type of business people would be in the field that they'd like to work in. My suggestion to the ladies was to have business cards printed with their names and contact information, then take their business cards and multiple copies of their resumes to *networking* events. In this way they could meet people who would be prospective employers or receive referrals from the business people in attendance.

Attending *networking* events for job search offers a way for you to meet prospective employers in a more relaxed setting outside of the typical traditional interview. This turns the tables and allows you to meet and "interview" the prospective employer, and they won't even realize it! You'll see and feel the corporate culture that the representative or boss portrays before the interview process at their office. This will allow you to see if this is a company that you would want to be affiliated with or work for and if they are a good fit for what you are looking for.

*Networking* makes your job search easier. You'll be working smarter, not harder, to find that dream job or career.

# NUGGET #10

## Public Relations Opens the Door to Successful Networking

### Introduction by Debra Pope

In the same way that "*networking* warms up a cold call," Public Relations warms up your *networking*. When you walk into a *networking* event and your name is already familiar to the participants there, you have a leg up for meeting the people you want to meet.

My favorite Public Relations guru is Jeff Crilley. When I ask people at a *networking* event, "Do you know Jeff Crilley?" more often than not the answer is, "Yes, he's a friend of mine."

Jeff is everyone's pal. He spends his time teaching business people how to get free publicity. Every time I hear him make a presentation at an event, I learn more valuable, usable tips to utilize the media to get free public relations.

I'm honored to have his input and valuable information in my business and in this book.

Now, with great pleasure, I'd like to introduce my pal, Jeff Crilley.

Jeff Crilley spent 25 years in TV news reporting in Dallas, Minneapolis, Omaha and Lansing.

He's made hundreds of national news appearances including CNN, CNN Headline News, FOX News, The Discovery Channel, Good Morning America and The CBS Early Show.

He was recognized by his peers with dozens of national and regional awards including the Emmy, the National Headliners Award, the Edward R. Murrow Award, the Thurgood Marshall Award and in 2004 was named by the Texas Associated Press, "The Best TV Reporter in the state." He retired from the news business in 2008 to start the world's first "all journalist" PR firm. For more information visit: www.RealNewsPR.com

**Real News PR**
**Millennium Tower**
**15455 N. Dallas Pkwy**
**Suite 750**
**Addison, TX 75001**
**(972) 865-2617**
**www.RealNewsPR.com**

# Public Relations Opens the Door to Successful Networking

by Jeff Crilley

Do you have a great idea for a story, but no clue how to get it in the news? Are you tired of pitching press releases the news media simply ignores? After 25 years of beating the street as a TV reporter, I have a scoop for you: the media needs good stories. But most stories are pitched so poorly; they are lost in the blizzard of faxes that blanket every newsroom.

So here are some insider secrets to getting covered on the news that even some PR pros don't know:

**Be Unusual**

The old adage about "Man bites dog" still holds true. The news doesn't cover what's normal. We cover the abnormal. PR whiz Carolyn Alvey knew this when she was trying to raise money for a charity several years ago. Instead of holding a garage sale, she sent out a press release announcing a "Celebrity Garage Sale." Everything from Bob Hope's old golf clubs to Roger Staubach's long-neglected neckties was for sale. By making an ordinary garage sale extraordinary, the media was instantly sold on the story.

**Tie into Feeding Frenzy**

Sometimes it's just a matter of asking yourself, "What will the media be buying?" Harry Potter is a great example. For the last few J.K. Rowling releases, I've found myself reporting live from local bookstores, interviewing children dressed in costume about how they can't wait until the stroke of midnight so they can get their hands on the next installment. Hold a Harry Potter party, complete with a costume contest, on the weekend of the next release and you'll have a parking lot full of news trucks.

**Choose the Right Reporter**

Perhaps the most common mistake even some PR pros make is trying to sell a good story to the wrong person. Most reporters have a specialty, like "crime" or "business." So seek out the reporter who will have the most to benefit from your story. Start studying the news. Before you call a TV station or try and pitch to the paper, become familiar with a reporter's work. Most of your stories will probably be feature stories. You'll want to pitch it to the reporter who enjoys warm, fuzzy pieces.

**Write Like a Reporter**

If I were going to send a press release to a reporter, I'd write the kind of headline that a newspaper would run. And I'd make the rest of the release so conversational that a TV anchor could read it right on the air. Why is this so important? A major market newsroom gets hundreds of press releases every day. Often the decision whether to cover your story is made in a matter of seconds. Many times that well-crafted sentence in the third paragraph of your press release is never read.

**Wait for a Slow News Day**

The holidays are the slowest "news times" of the year. When government offices are closed, so are most of our sources. Take advantage of it. In fact, take out your calendar and begin circling government holidays and the days surrounding government holidays. If the government is coasting into a long holiday weekend, so is the rest of the country. That's when we reporters are scrambling to find something to cover. Pitch even an average story on a day when the media is starving for news, and you're much more likely to get coverage.

**Flattery will get you everywhere**

When you call a journalist on the phone, the best opening line there is goes like this: "Can I tell you how much I love your work?" All reporters have egos. We like to believe you faithfully watch our reports or clip our articles from the paper and hang them on your refrigerator. When you call us and give us sincere and specific compliments, we think we have a fan on the phone. Our guard is down. We don't know we're about to be pitched. But more importantly, you are communicating something very important to the journalist. You're saying, "I know who you are, what you do, and why you're the best person for this story." You'd be surprised at how many people will call a TV reporter and ask, "Now, are you the person who is on camera or are you behind the scenes?" That's a very bad pitch.

**Thank You Notes**

After the story airs or is printed in the paper, send a thank you note for the coverage. That simple gesture goes a long way. But it amazes me how few people take the time to do it. I'd say only one out of every hundred people I put on the news ever bothers to call or write and thank me. And it shouldn't stop there. Take an interest in the reporters and the stories they cover. Later you might want to drop them a note for no reason other than to compliment them on a good report. Tell them you're always keeping your eye out for other good stories to give them. It keeps your name in front of them and continues to build good will.

There you go. Now you're armed with knowledge that even some well-paid public relations professions don't practice. If your idea is unique, visual, and pitched to the right person when the supply of news is running thin, you're in!

# NUGGET #10 continued

## Public Relations Opens the Door to Successful *Networking*

Public Relations plays such a big part in your *networking*, I feel it's appropriate to have two experts address the topic.

The next expert I'd like to introduce, Jeanie Douthitt, is a prime example of how helping more people is rewarding both spiritually, intellectually and financially. After attending a mind expanding eWomenNetwork conference a few years ago, she came up with an idea of how to help single women achieve the American Dream: owning a home.

After 20 years in Information Technology at IBM, Jeanie entered real estate and was named to the Coldwell Banker International Diamond Society. She's the founder of "Smart Women Buy Homes," a program that helps single women through the entire home-buying process. Jeanie's philosophy is to provide her clients with the highest level of professionalism, tenacity, focus and passion for making dreams come true. In 2007 - 2009 she was named to the President's Circle and recently awarded **#1 Top Individual Sales Associate for 2009** for Coldwell Banker Apex, Realtors. She works with buyers, sellers, builders, developers and investors.

**Jeanie Douthitt**
**Coldwell Banker Realty**
**jeanie.dothitt@coldwellbanker.com**
972-208-8797

# Defining Public Relations and How to Use it in *Networking*

By Jeanie Douthitt

What exactly is Public Relations, or PR? Public relations is about doing something newsworthy that you want to communicate and then telling your audience what you have done. Today that is done through many different mediums. It can be simple and done through email campaigns, Facebook, Twitter, blogs, mailings etc. Or it could be done traditionally such as TV, radio, press releases, newspaper, speaking engagements, *networking* events and many others. As a business owner, you need to figure out what types of PR are right for you.

Personally, I have done many of these. Some worked, while some worked better than others. Being in sales for many years, I found what worked best for me, and what I liked best was *networking*. *Networking* takes dedication and a love for meeting new people. *Networking* is not for everyone. Like many other forms of PR, it might not result in a sale today. It is more about building a personal relationship and then the business will follow. *Networking* is all about "showing up," being prepared to tell your story and your success. In turn, you need to listen to what others are sharing about themselves, looking for opportunities to help them. Believe it or not, it is not all about YOU! I know from my own experience that the most success comes from the attitude of "how can I help you?"

You also need to be comfortable in your own shoes. *Networking* is hard for a lot of people. Sometimes you have to step outside of your comfort zone, embrace new people and be the one to reach out to start a new relationship. You will not be an overnight success, but even meeting one new person is a big step. The next time will be much easier, and eventually you won't remember how difficult it was the first time.

## Find Your Primary Drive

I worked at IBM for many years and although I had many great jobs and worked hard, I realized I had no burning passion for my job. When I finally became comfortable with taking the next step, I took a leap of faith and moved into real estate. Why? Because I found a passion and a mission only real estate could help me accomplish. That passion was to help single women buy homes. Just because you are single doesn't mean you can't live the American Dream of home ownership. It became a mission of mine when my friends and I had difficultly navigating through the process of owning a home on our own. Story after story inspired me to create a program to help single women.

The second step for me was to partner with both a mortgage and a title company who had the same values: dedication and professionalism in helping single women achieve the dream of home ownership. Initially, the name of my program, SWAT (Single Women As A Team), did not help convey what it did. I had not envisioned how far I wanted my mission to reach. I started thinking small and then realized I wanted to go bigger. When I attended an eWomenNetwork conference, I soon understood how immense this opportunity could be. Women from all over the United States wanted to know if this type of program was available in their area. When the conference was over, I immediately started talking with Coldwell Banker about the need for a national program. After eighteen months of working with them, there is now a national program for Realtors to help single women. Coldwell Banker did extensive research and homework before investing in marketing materials and developing the new program. This proved to me that there was a market for single women. It also gave me a national brand and credibility that you get from a large company that has been in business for over 100 years. This is exactly what I had hoped for. Again, this shows how important it is just to show up and utilize your network.

## Public Relations versus Anything Else

Traditional *networking* has done a lot for my business, and I truly enjoy it. I have been doing it long enough to have seen some people hit a ceiling. I found myself getting to that point. I felt that if I was going to take my business to the next level, I needed the expertise of a PR professional. I was very hesitant at first to make that move. As a business owner, it is always very hard to relinquish any aspect of my business to other people.

Trust is essential to being successful. People have to trust me and I have to trust others in return. It is just good business knowing you can't do everything alone, if you want to continue to grow. Coming from a large corporation who had deep pockets and its own PR team, it was very scary to take this big step as a small business owner. However, I knew if I wanted to continue to grow my business, it was necessary.

At the end of 2009 I was ready to start working with a PR company. I chose someone who came highly recommended who was instrumental in helping another business in my industry become a recognized name. When I started working with Zazza Media Strategies it was suggested that I make several changes. The new brand was created and "Smart Women Buy Homes" was born, with a new logo, website and other marketing materials to promote my services, my expertise and my network. I was now ready for PR.

The truth is that anyone can build their own brand and have their own team of experts. The myth that PR is extremely expensive is not true. Stay dedicated and true to your goals for your business and the rest will follow.

Shortly after Smart Women Buy Homes was launched, I was featured on the 10 o'clock news. After the first one came another one, and then several after that. I had morning show segments, was interviewed as an expert for stories, had features—and the list goes on. I wasn't a TV star but I was "The Expert" on all things concerning single women buying homes. I was commanding the time of a news broadcast and that meant many things. My mission was being validated and I gained immense credibility. Ultimately, I was meeting a realistic expectation that included local prominence, recognition and stature.

It is not about being overwhelmed by media coverage but rather the diversity in coverage you receive. Why? Shortly after one of the first feature stories I was eating lunch and out of nowhere, I was approached by a young woman. She recognized me from the story. She did not remember the name of the program but she knew about it. At that time it became evident to me that my network was larger than it was before. My personal network now included people I had never met because of PR.

**The Practical Results of PR**

The door had literally been pushed opened to many new opportunities. Not only had my network grown exponentially after the media exposure, but I was now rising in the ranks of the networks I already belonged to.

PR has networked back to me. It has given me more creditability. This credibility confirms that I am a viable Realtor and I have a viable product. I have seen doors open because more and more people are willing to introduce me to others. Over time, I don't think PR would have worked without the element of *networking*. After the first story, if I had stopped PR, the results would not have been the same. *Networking*, complemented by PR, has taken me to the next level.

This past April, in the midst of a recession, I saw my largest month in my six years since starting in Real Estate. In that month 75% of all closed transactions were with single women. I can credit the new business to the media and PR exposure. PR is a perfect complement to the work I have already done and continue to do. It is not just for big companies but for any business wanting to grow.

No, I haven't made it on the Oprah Show but because of PR and my *networking* relationships, but one never knows what door may open next. Any business owner can use and benefit from PR; it's not just for the Fortune 500 companies. I can't tell you how much I have learned and benefited since I started using PR and *networking* together. *Networking* is essential, even though the idea of putting yourself out there can be daunting. The best advice I can give anyone who is just starting the process is to "just do it." Take the plunge. Putting yourself out there can be hard the first time, but it gets easier. Confidence comes with experience!

Just as my Grandma Moses said, "Life is what we make it—always has been, always will be."

# NUGGET #11

## Building Relationships
### *"Giving First, Sharing Always"*

### Introduction by Debra Pope

Four years ago in Plano, TX I attended an eWomenNetwork event for the first time. I have always loved *Networking* events, and the excitement, the electricity and energy that I get from other people who want to meet me as much as I want to meet them. I sensed from the very first moment that eWomenNetwork was a different organization from any other I had ever experienced. The event theme and philosophy was "Giving First, and Sharing Always." I joined on the spot. Sandra Yancey sets the tone of the organization as coming from a place of abundance and sharing with others. She is a dynamic leader of women and one whom I'm proud to say I know and admire. It's my pleasure to introduce Sandra Yancey.

Sandra Yancey is the Founder & CEO of eWomenNetwork, with chapters all across the United States and Canada. She is the recipient of numerous business awards, including Excellence in Leadership from the Euro-American Women's Council in Athens, Greece, the Entrepreneur Star Award from Microsoft, the Woman Advocate of the Year Award from the Women's Regional Publishing Association and the Distinguished Women's Award from Northwood University.

She is recognized as an American Hero by CNN for mobilizing resources for the girl's high school basketball team of Pass Christian, Mississippi after Hurricane Katrina's devastation. Philanthropy is at the core of Sandra's personal mission, and her eWomenNetwork Foundation awards hundreds of thousands of dollars to nonprofit organizations that help women and children.

Sandra is the author of *Relationship Networking: The Art of Turning Contacts Into Connections.* She is the co-creator and producer of the movie The GLOW Project.

**Sandra Yancey**
**eWomenNetwork**
**Sandra.Yancey@eWomenNetwork.net**
**972-620-9995**

## Relationship Networking is an Attitude, Not a Destination

At one time a powerful business person was defined by his or her ability to acquire external things—fancy titles and corner offices, large staffs and fat expense accounts. But the rules have changed. Today, powerful has been replaced by influential. Influential people are defined by their ability to make things happen and get things done. How do they do this? They build solid relationship networks based on four key elements. First of all, they strategically seek out people and look for ways to establish an introduction. What may look like a coincidental meeting to the rest of the world is part of an intentional effort of navigating through the *networking* process, which is to converse, connect, collaborate, and create.

Each one of these elements requires relationship skills. For example, to begin to converse with someone, you need to be able to start a conversation by asking questions that invite information and disclosure. Then, as the person is providing this information, you look for opportunities to connect by identifying common ground. Common ground consists of ways in which you can relate. It could be creating a linkage to another person you know, or a hobby you share, or a place you both vacationed, or a dilemma or challenge you both have experienced. Next, you see opportunities to collaborate. An example could be by informing the person about a great book and how it helped you with a similar issue.

Savvy networkers will follow up and follow through by sending their copy or buying the person her own. Finally, this relationship in time—some sooner, some later, and some never—will lend itself to the opportunity to create. This might occur when you "create" yet another new relationship by putting the person and someone else in contact with each other. In this case, your role is to initiate the conversation and create the connection. Once this is established, two savvy business women will take your lead from that point on. The end result? You will have woven the web of connections known as "a thriving network."

Those with thriving networks are in a position to make things happen easily and fluidly. They remember people they meet—their names, what they do, and how to reach them. Perhaps more importantly, they remember the hearts of conversations and the needs of those they talk to. They are constantly on the lookout for solutions to those needs, whether that turns out to be a good book, another person or an invitation to an important event. Powerful people make it their "business" to actually follow up and follow through with these connections, and in so doing differentiate themselves from the merely well-intentioned. When someone assists them, influential people send a hand-written thank-you note. They understand the subtle but oh-so-meaningful differences these touches make in today's technology-dependent society, which has come to expect that a quick e-mail will suffice. Relationship networkers know that it is by connecting the right people with the right challenges and opportunities that companies, careers, and lives are built and made better.

There is a three-letter word that, when scrambled and rearranged, describes the art of turning contacts into connections. That word is **how**. Rearranged, it becomes so much more important to know who rather than know how. The 21st century has ushered in a whole host of new realities and, the truth is, with the pace at which things are changing, you will never to able to know how to do everything. Those days are long gone, and they will never return. You can constantly grow your knowledge by knowing who to call, the person who will know what you need to know. My point here is, despite all you've read about the power of technology and all it can do to enhance your success, it will forever pale in comparison to the power of relationships and all that they can do to enhance your success.

The art of relationship *networking* boils down to your ability to communicate effectively and purposefully with the right people. The best St. John suit or four-color business cards won't work for you if you don't learn how to express yourself with confidence, conviction, and compassion. Couple these attributes with the ability to make others feel comfortable by mastering the arts of listening and conversation, and you have the recipe for building solid connections.

**Belief in Abundance**

Relationship networkers come from a perspective of abundance. Their intention is to share information, not merely gather information for their personal use or withhold information as a means of demonstrating power. To establish a growing and evolving relationship network, you must first recognize, believe, and behave according to the philosophy: "It takes teamwork to make the dream work." It is through the spirit of abundance that you demonstrate your own character and integrity by helping others whenever you can. After all, how can you expect others to do for you what you are not first willing to do for them? The point is that real relationship networkers live the law of the universe: You must give in order to receive.

You know, at a deep level, that when you give freely and without expectations, others will be there for you when you need them most. If you come from a place of scarcity, that is exactly what you will attract. I believe you become the sum average of the five people you hang around with most. I've often used this philosophy as my own guidepost when learning about others. Most people spend time with others who are a lot like them, so take inventory of those with whom you surround yourself. Are they coming from a place of abundance? Do they freely and willingly give to others, sharing information? If you are not getting the answers you desire, then you have one important decision to make: change your relationships. You can literally change your life when you change your relationships.

Asking to share something as simple as a recipe can be an eye-opening experience. I never understand women who say, "I would love to give it to you, but this recipe is a family secret." There is no place in this world for such limited thinking! How does it help you to hoard a family recipe? Does the food taste better, or nurture your family more because your friends can't make the dish exactly as you do? My mother always told me that the way to develop a real legacy is to share all that you can with others—even favorite family recipes! Now imagine how valued your friend will feel when you've chosen to share that special recipe with her. She will feel so valued, she may share her best recipe (or even her next $1 million contract opportunity) with you.

Relationship networkers know that it is by connecting the right people with the right challenges and opportunities that companies, careers, and lives are built and made better.

The old saying, "You have to give in order to receive," has never been truer than when used in the context of relationship *networking*. You have to believe that *networking* is about sharing, and expect that it will not be an even exchange at first. As you look for ways to help others, trust that others will be looking for ways to help you. One thing I know for sure, if you are too busy to help others achieve success by helping them overcome tough challenges or access transformational opportunities, then you're just too busy, period. Keep focused on the larger picture, understanding that some of our greatest rewards aren't instant. Trust that the universe knows when you need its help most. It always shows up—not a minute early or a minute late.

Make time each day to pause and reflect on the numbers of times you have used my favorite five-word question: "How can I help you?" Consider the new connections, friends, and relationships you have established. Finish each day knowing that adopting an attitude of support and service will lead to an incurable epidemic of abundance. Think of every instance that you have assisted another in accomplishing her goals and dreams as a seed you have planted in your *networking* garden, then patiently watch the flowers bloom. Make no mistake about it, your network equals your power. Your power is determined by the amount of influence you have to get things accomplished.

## Anytime, Anywhere is the Right Time and Place to Network

So many people think they need to find the right place to network. There is no one right place, because you take *networking* with you wherever you go. *Networking* is something that you do along the journey of life. *Networking* is a lifestyle you can practice anywhere and everywhere. Whether you are at an event, a restaurant, a nail or hair salon, an association meeting, in a checkout line, or on an airplane, there is an opportunity to network, an opportunity to converse, connect, collaborate and create. It becomes part of you. You have to say to yourself, "I'm going to hang in there and be fine, even though not every interaction is going to be fruitful and provide results." But if you hang in there, the next time might bear fruit. You are planting seeds, and you never know which seeds will sprout.

*Networking* can be like going to church or exercising: It requires fortitude to get going, it feels so good when you're finished, and it always produces long-term benefits and results. You just have to network, make it a way of life, and experiment with it. Give yourself a chance to make mistakes, learn from those mistakes, move on and try again. Remember that *networking* is a skill and, like all skills to be mastered, it takes practice. And the more you practice, the better you get. In time, you will be able to turn yourself from an amateur to a pro.

There is a lot less luck in life than we think. I'm not saying that luck doesn't play a part in success, but I do think we give it way too much credit. The universe works much more deliberately that we can possibly fathom. Luck often emerges in direct proportion to the consistent and deliberate attention we place on developing key skills and competencies. Developing relationships and growing your network takes time and intention. Trust that in the process you will see the impact *networking* will have on your career and business. Again, remember that everyone who makes it has a slew of wonderful connections and relationships that have been developed by "Giving First, and Sharing Always."

# NUGGET #11 continued

## Relationship Networking
### *"Giving First, Sharing Always"*

My position with eWomenNetwork has led me to many women of great influence. Yet these women have big hearts and these women who put others first. One of the most wonderful women, who has had the biggest impression on me, is Jo-Ann Vacing, Executive Managing Director for eWomenNetwork for several Western Canadian cities. She devotes her life to serving the women in those areas of Western Canada, brining motivation and excitement in the events she produces there.

Her outstanding devotion has earned her the title of Executive Managing Director of the Year for eWomenNetwork for 2009. While in a small package, and younger than me, she's like my big sister, my "Femtor." I'm always amazed at what she accomplishes in growing membership and for fund raising for

the eWomenNetwork Foundation. I'm thrilled to introduce to you Jo-Ann Vacing.

**Jo-Ann Vacing eWomenNetwork**
**Executive Managing Director Alberta**
jo-annvacing@ewomennetwork.com
**Phone 403 274 3319**
**Fax 403 233 0899**

Jo-Ann Vacing, eWomenNetwork
Managing Director of the Year, 2009

# Are you the Dating or Marrying Type of Networker?

**The similarities are uncanny:**

***Dating***: When we date, we look for someone we would like to spend time with—someone who has similar interests, is respectful, has integrity, and is trustworthy. We want someone who is interested in us and who enhances our life—someone we would be happy to introduce to others.

***Networking***: As a business owner, I have the honor and privilege of working with clients I like to spend time with, who have similar interests, who are respectful, who are interested in assisting others, and who have impact in business and community, who have integrity, who I refer to others with confidence, who I trust.

If we agree in principle that *Networking* is like dating, why then would we expect to build a business relationship without laying a foundation? Why, on the first date, are we looking for a ring when what we need to begin with is a coffee?

The basics of dating are the basics of networking:
- Image and presentation (you have only one chance to make a first impression)…
- Asking relevant questions (not interrogating with hot lights)
- Listening and taking interest (we all want to be heard)

When out on your first date, these are questions you should stay clear of:
- How soon can we announce our engagement?
- When is a good time to go house hunting?
- How many children do you want?

Of course, if we want to end the date, those are great questions!

The same could be said about asking someone you have just met the following:

- Can I come by this week so we can sign the paperwork?
- We have the perfect product/service for you. Can I have your Visa to get you started?

If we want a second date (a chance to build the relationship), we must provide the value.

How?

Be consistent, show up and connect to others—after all, *networking* is about building long-term relationships with IMPACT!

*Networking* is an effective and useful process in growing your business. *Networking* can be accomplished in a variety of ways and is not limited to formal functions. If done by design, *networking* will significantly impact your business.

Here are some common misconceptions about organized *networking*:

All businesses must join at least five organizations to see results.

Results are not determined by the number of organizations you join, but rather by the type and fit of the organizations.

Some things to consider:

Is there a link to your ideal client, whether direct or indirect?

What is the retention rate of the organization? Retention is critical because the opportunity to build long-term profitable relationships is directly impacted, and therefore so are your results!

Diversity in the group can also have significant impact—if there are too many of the same businesses, nobody benefits.

Further, what are the demographics of the members, and even more important what are the psychographics of the members?

All organizations that are truly connected to their members are able to share this information.

All organizations are equal and do the same things.

Not so!

The mission of some organizations is to provide personal and professional development. Others are referral groups in which your role as a member is to provide referrals to other members on a weekly basis.

Some are there to support change in regulations; still others are created to assist others in the community through fundraising efforts.

When attending a *networking* event I must hand out all my business cards, gather theirs, and email them my information. Further, I can expect to do business right away with at least ten people from each event I attend.

Not so!

Business cards should not be dealt indiscriminately like a deck of cards, but rather handed to those individuals who would like to learn more about you and can assist you.

The most successful businesses I know practice giving to others first.

*Networking* works best when I participate regularly. Simply showing up is not a measure of success.

Results are more accurately measured by the types of interactions you have. Therefore, the results you garner will be a direct reflection of your efforts, including your follow-through.

# NUGGET #12

## Networking To Build Your Database

By Debra Pope

For small to mid-size companies, the most effective way of advertising is one or more methods of "direct contact" advertising. They need a database to make the direct contact advertising for direct mail flyers, coupon mailers, e-mails, or to use social media.

Many small business people know that direct contact advertising is the best and most economical method of advertising. The mistake they make is in the way that they acquire the names, addresses and miscellaneous contact info to do direct mail.

They purchase expensive mailing lists to build their database to do their direct contact advertising by e-mail or US mail.

Some business people use the list of Chamber Members in their community to build their database for their direct contact advertising.

The most successful way to reach your customers is by the oldest method since time began. That method is still the same as in days of old and that is by word of mouth. Word of mouth advertising comes to you by referral of a happy, satisfied existing client or customer. Or the word of mouth client or customer can come to you because you have met that potential client or customer in person through

*Networking.*

Hands down, the best way to reach people who are your potential customers is through *networking.*

Through *networking,* having met the potential client or customer in person, and assuming you make a favorable impression, they will begin to seek you and your services because of the establishment of trust and confidence.

Everyone wants and needs to buy from someone they know, trust and respect. Having seen you, met you and connected with you, they will begin to trust you.

*Networking* enhances and positively impacts direct contact methods and direct mail methods. The more high tech we become, the more we use technology, the more **valuable** up close, face to face, personal, high touch marketing becomes. Human beings have a need for personal, in-person contact.

If someone has met you in person, they are less likely to throw away or dismiss the direct mail piece you send them.

They are less likely to delete your e-mail marketing if they've met you in person.

They are also less likely to dismiss your Facebook, Twitter, LinkedIn or Plaxo if they've met you in person.

Thus, a valuable part of your business plan should be to build your database by *networking.*

Through the business cards you receive, you should begin to build your database, which will become the cornerstone and foundation for all future methods of advertising you will use in your business.

**Refer to Business Card Management outlined in Nugget #6**.

Use the business cards you have received to build your database.

There are several different software programs you can use to build your business database. The ones I prefer I are Microsoft Outlook and Microsoft Excel.

When I return to my office after a *networking* event I immediately send an e-mail to the people I feel are my target market, and from the e-mail I send I create a contact in Outlook. Then I create a Distribution List of the event attendees or add the individual's contact information into an existing Distribution List. I make as many notes on the contact information as I can to help me remember the person for future correspondence with the new prospective customer/clients.

Another software program you may want to use is Card Scan. With Card Scan you feed individual business cards you've received one at a time through the scanner. Card Scan has its own database program, or you can set up the software to take the scanned card and place it in Outlook.

You can use your Yahoo account, Gmail account or whatever contact software system you are the most familiar with or are comfortable with. The important thing is to build the database and use it to ensure your contact marketing is a success and not a waste of time, resources and your money.

It's very important to record present customers or clients into your database as well. Research shows it takes 10 times as much time and money to find a new customer as to keep your present customer/clients.

Your database is worth its weight in gold.

If and when you decide to seek investors in your business or it's time to sell your business, one of the selling points of your company is your database and client list.

Personal contact made through *networking* is the most rewarding, efficient and valuable method of database building.

# NUGGET #13

## Your Network = Your Net Worth

### Introduction by Debra Pope

In our previous Chapters/Nuggets we've mentioned that it's not always what you know, but who you know that allows you to reach ever-elusive success at a much faster pace.

*Networking* sets the stage for you to work smarter, not harder. Who you've met through your *networking* does without a doubt influence your success.

The lady I'm about to introduce to you is another example of a woman who knows how to mine gold by investing in the people she meets, combined with dedication to her business, a great heart and brilliant business sense.

Linda owns a beautiful retail storefront business called Elegant Essentials. She is also the Executive Managing Director of the Knoxville, Tennessee Chapter, achieving Executive Managing Director in record breaking time.

She is a "Femtor" to all women she comes in contact with.

Linda truly knows that her Network = Her Net Worth.

I'm proud to introduce Linda Parrent.

Linda Parrent follows her dreams. Linda, an accomplished master florist and certified interior decorator, relocated from Arkansas to Tennessee to launch *Elegant Essentials Home Décor and Gifts* "from scratch." The career move has garnered Parrent and her store numerous "Woman to Watch" and "Best Gift Shop" awards.

In 2010, Linda added Managing Director of the Knoxville Chapter of eWomenNetwork to her resume. That same year, she was featured in the July issue of *Woman's Day*.

Linda is actively engaged in her community through Chambers of Commerce and local non-profits. She and her husband Stephen have three children. Linda enjoys traveling, cookbooks, and time spent with friends and family.

**Elegant Essentials**
**www.ShopElegantEssentials.com**
**linda@ShopElegantEsssentials.com**
**865-247-0157**
**eWomenNetwork**
**Managing Director**
**www.eWomenNetwork.com**
**lindaparrent@eWomenNetwork.com**
**865-765-8540**

# Your Network = Your Net Worth

### By Linda Parrent

I've been in retail business in one aspect or another—clerk, manager, buyer, and now owner of my own boutique—over 20 years. I was taught, as we all were, that if you find the best location, sell quality products, offer superior customer service, and hang an "open" sign on your door, customers will come. Not today. Now, you must get actively involved in bringing the customer to you.

So how do you change everything you have been taught? With practice and time, you will evolve into a confident and trustworthy networker. It makes sense, right? Then why not start right now?

## CHANGE WITH THE TIMES

In the past most retail business owners never left their shops. It was difficult for me, too, until I saw the value of *networking*. People were making a connection to me and, in turn, to my business. *This is really important: you are your product!*

We can purchase goods or services from anyone. There is a reason customers come to you; it is **you**. Deal with that fact! I know it is hard as women to understand that you are the one they have a connection to. That is why someone will go out of their way to get your product or service and bypass everyone else.

The times have changed and we have to change with them. We have to get out there and bring customers into our stores. Don't be afraid to re-invent yourself and your business. That will keep you ahead of everyone else who chooses to remain stagnant.

## ONE STEP AT A TIME

To take that first step, leave your location.

I know; you could "miss a customer, a call, a vendor – yada, yada, yada." I made all the excuses, too! It was hard at first to justify leaving my comfort zone, my domain, my kingdom, my store. But, when I started to see the benefits, all became clear in my mind.

There are several ways to start at your first *networking* event. I suggest you have a fellow networker go with you. Trust me, they are out there and are very eager to have a guest at an event. Let them show you the ropes and help you get a feel for what *networking* is all about. This fellow networker is going to be someone who knows you and your business, and vice versa. At this event, your partner is going to introduce you to her contacts and share stories of your accomplishments. You, in turn, will do the same for her. This way you don't have to talk about yourself initially; they do it for you, and the door is open. It is much easier to let someone else talk about your talents than for you to boast about yourself.

We were raised as women to believe that the ones who talked about themselves were "stuck up," "big headed," and "conceited." Well, in the networking world, we have to talk about ourselves. So, get over it! But remember…

*Networking and selling are not the same.*

No one wants to be "sold" at a *networking* event. They will run—that's why, when *networking*, I don't sell. Do not push your product or service on someone; you will push your opportunities away.

Passion for what you do should never appear as aggression. Passion draws interest! Start with a little spark; this will lead to the fire you ignite in others around you. Everyone wants to be part of the excitement! Create excitement and you will get interest.

Observe other people at the event to learn *networking* do's and don'ts. You never just want to be in the game, you want to be *on top of your game*. Rise above the crowd, and the buzz will start. Customers will come to you after time because of the buzz from your fellow networkers.

**ELEVATOR SPEECH**

This is the quick introduction you can present anywhere when you talk about your business. This is key; so take a little time to think about what you do and how it will have interest and appeal when someone else hears it.

You only need one sentence to spark interest. Example: "I provide people with a sensory experience." Does that say I have a boutique? No!

The next question someone usually asks me is, "what do you do?" Now I have permission to talk about my business, because they have expressed interest. Practice, practice, practice with someone you trust who is a seasoned networker. Let them give you honest advice on where you need improvement. Simple, right?

**BUSINESS CARDS**

Simple, but true, always have business cards. You have the opportunity to network everywhere—at church, the grocery store, even the doctor's office. It's limitless. But if you don't have a business card, do you think they are going to remember all the wonderful information about you and your business? I will tell you the answer: no.

Never give someone another step to do. Example: "I ran out of business cards, you can check out my website online." This individual has a life, too. Do you think they are going to go home and jump on the computer because you ran out of cards? Maybe, but I doubt it.

Also remember to get your customer's business card or contact information, and offer to follow up with them during the week. Once you start the process, it will flow. The more you do it, the easier it gets.

**STOP AND LISTEN**

This is key to all good *networking*! If we are so busy thinking about what we are going to say, are we even listening to what someone else is saying? How can we build our business if we never listen?

If a customer comes into my store and tells me in the first sentence she is looking for a candle for a friend, that's easy, right? Well, not if I am not listening. So I tell her about all the new handbags, scarves, chocolates, and on and on. She is now frustrated that I did not hear her initial request, and I potentially lose a customer. Now, if I first show her all the candles I have available in a variety of scents and price ranges, I fulfilled what she is looking for and she is happy. This is the time to tell her about all the other wonderful things she might have a need or interest in. I took the time to listen and have shown an interest in her needs.

Remember: "How can I help you?"

## RELATIONSHIPS - THE GOLDEN RULE

We become the best networkers we can because we have built relationships with other networkers. Relationships take time and don't happen overnight. Your business didn't happen overnight either, and you were willing to put in the time, right?

Trust and commitment are very easy to accomplish, but who do we trust? Start trusting in you and your ability. The more confident you are about *who you are* and *what you believe in*, the easier it is to build relationships. Building relationships builds business.

I was taught if you can't say something nice, don't. Treat others as you would like to be treated. When you help others, it comes back tenfold. So, why do we make *networking* harder than it is? You don't have to try hard to build relationships.

Learn about someone's business "beyond the business." Ask how you can help their business. When you do this, and follow through with it, you start becoming a trusted networker. It won't be long before everyone knows. This starts peeling the layers, and lets you learn, not only about their business, but about them—their interests, hobbies, families and so on. This makes you a stronger networker when you can talk about someone's human side, too.

We all have the same issues—different faces, but same issues. I'm never afraid to make a mistake and show I am not perfect. We all need help or we would not be *networking*. Why would I be doing it if I had all the business and resources that I need?

Remember that everyone at these events is a version of you, just in different bodies with different business, but all the same! *Be yourself.* I can't stress this enough! We want to know you and build a relationship with you, not the mask that you put on when you attend an event. Remember, we want to do business with **you**.

## YOUR BEST ADVERTISMENT…

…Is you! No one can market your business like you can. I advertise in the newspaper, magazines, radio, and television at one time of the year or another. But if I did not actively network my business, the advertising wouldn't work. By being out in the public with other networkers who are in all parts of town, I make my business come alive. People get to know my personality, my passion, my drive. Then, when someone sees an ad for my store, they have a true connection to me and my business.

We all want to be connected! Just because we live in a point-and-click society does not mean we can thrive without human contact. Remember that you are your business; we need to know you!

Start one step at a time and you will eventually build an army of networkers for **you**.

# NUGGET #14

## Climbing The "Pyramid of Success" Against All Odds

### Introduction by Debra Pope

Dr. Virginia Wells is a woman of great accomplishment and great caring. I'm amazed at her wit, intelligence, warmth and concern. She is one of the most eloquent writers I've known. She is my business coach and friend. I owe her more than I can ever repay.

Her "Pyramid of Success" plan will allow we who follow her teachings to rise to greatness more than we ever imagined by serving others on boards of not for profit organizations. Then, this will lead to serving as highly paid directors for major fortune 500 corporations.

Now, I'd like to introduce you, my friend, my business coach, Dr. Virginia Wells.

Dr. Virginia Trevizo Wells is the president of Organizational Behavior Consulting and Training (OBC&T) based out of Dallas, TX. OBC&T focuses on guiding small and medium size businesses to achieve their highest potential through executive coaching, innovative business strategic planning, and customized training. She combines her business experience and her academic research of successful business practices to create personalized solutions for her clients. The Greater Dallas Hispanic Chamber of Commerce hired her firm to teach entrepreneurial business members to launch their start-ups. She was successful in helping these small businesses increase revenues from 200 to 900%. Wells has served as a board member of numerous non-profit organizations and industry associations. Most recently she was the President of Peacemakers, Inc., an organization dedicated to promoting and educating people about Peace. She holds a Ph.D. in Organizational Systems from Saybrook University in San Francisco, CA.

**Dr. Virginia Wells, OBC&T**
**vwjunbug@yahoo.com**

## Climbing The "Pyramid of Success" Against All Odds

### By Dr. Virginia Trevizo Wells

Have you ever wondered how some people achieve great success when the odds are against them?

This is the story of a young businesswoman who is a rising star and is on the road to success despite all odds. She possesses a powerful trait that she utilizes on a daily basis that is largely unspoken of. It is a simple concept, which is often overlooked, yet critical to success in any career.

Before I start sharing this secret ingredient for a successful career, let me tell you the story of the young woman who has been climbing the pyramid of success for the last six years.

Like most entrepreneurs, this young woman started her company because she needed a job, so she decided to create it by opening up her own business. The odds were against her because she had limited experience in the field she chose, little money to invest in this new venture, and she lacked a bachelor degree. What she did possess was an intense desire to succeed, regardless of the personal sacrifice. She also was persistent and knew that if she gave up, her dream to better herself and her children would disappear.

Although a strong desire and persistence are critical elements to succeed in business, this chapter is about the additional third element that she unknowingly possessed, **being influential**. Our young businesswoman intuitively used influence to accelerate her earning potential and grow her business quickly. By following the simple steps outlined below you can also accelerate your business growth.

### *Level One: Chambers of Commerce*

Our young entrepreneur entered the pyramid of success at the broadest and lowest level of social networking by joining a local Chamber of Commerce. Like most business owners, she attended the events hosted by the Chamber expecting to get business, and what she ultimately received was visibility. *(Each level of the imagined pyramid has its reward for participation and this level's reward is visibility).*

Every new business owner needs visibility so others can become aware of their existence, and so they can start attracting business. The young entrepreneur entered the pyramid of success at the level where most start-up business owners also enter. However, her likeable demeanor soon propelled her business and moved her up the pyramid of success.

Being likeable (which is an aspect of being influential) caused other business people to give her advice on how to build her business quickly. Also, being a person of influence means that you are open to being influenced by others. The young entrepreneur allowed herself to be advised by those she trusted. They shared with her the importance of joining a professional organization. She found a professional organization that was in her industry and soon became a member. Thus she moved up into the second level of the pyramid.

### *Level Two: Professional Organizations*

Professional organizations and a smaller number of people inhabit the second level of the success pyramid. Usually business owners join organizations that mirror their industry. This young entrepreneur quickly learned that just being a professional member was not sufficient enough to build her business further. Instinctively she volunteered to become a chairperson in one of the organization's committees. This title brought her increased visibility and business because she took on a leadership role. Being in a position of leadership or authority is another form of influence.

The reason this type of influence works is because being a chairperson of a committee confers a level of formal power. The title implies responsibility, authority, and the ability to control resources. In fact, most people respond automatically by nature to whoever is in charge of the meeting.

Being in charge of the meetings and seeing to members' needs and wants increased the young entrepreneur's business to such extent that she was soon sought after to speak on her newfound success. Speaking at various organizations also heightened her influence, because people in the audience considered her an expert in the given topic. As an expert, she was sought after as someone to conduct business with and thereby her company grew even more.

Her due diligence and dedication to the professional organization became apparent, and people started offering to do favors for her. Unknowingly, she evoked the rule of reciprocity. According to Robert Cialdini, "The rule demands that one sort of action be reciprocated with a similar sort of action. A favor is to be met with another favor." Soon the young entrepreneur started to learn how to use reciprocity to her advantage, and her company grew again because people started referring business to her. *(This is the reward for this second level, growth by referrals).* People in the community started taking notice of this young entrepreneur's business savvy and soon she was asked to run for a board of directors' seat.

Most business owners, when confronted with this opportunity, shy away from it because of the amount of responsibility it implies. The young entrepreneur's strong desire to succeed outweighed her aversion to assuming more responsibility. It was at this point that she hired me to coach her on how to communicate and network more effectively. I also shared with her recommendations on how to navigate this new leadership position she was about to undertake. Full of resolve to overcome her fear of public speaking, she decided to move forward. It was at this point that she expanded her earning capacity even more and soon became a rising star.

### *Level Three: Non-profit Board of Directors*

This third level is where you typically see rising stars. These rising stars figure out that in order to grow and expand their businesses, they need to meet people who occupy different social networks. For the young entrepreneur, becoming a non-profit board member gave her the perfect platform for meeting a variety of new people. It was challenging at first because there were people who had different family and educational backgrounds, new social circles that encompassed varied professions, different lifestyles, and new geographical locations. She now was encountering a whole new world. The bonus to this scenario is that the broad network with many acquaintances represents a strong source of access to decision makers. *(The reward for the third level is access to key decision makers, a key ingredient for business growth)*.

In this level of the success pyramid, the rule of reciprocity is a critical element to utilize. The numbers are few and the competition is stronger. The young entrepreneur continued to use reciprocity to grow her business and currently she is laying the foundation for entering the fourth level of the pyramid by developing her personal power.

Personal power is the power you have after the powers of position and relationship are taken away. It is based on qualities that others recognize within you. They include trustworthiness, relating well to others, expertise of high value to others, an ability to communicate opinions and ideas in compelling ways, and accomplishments that merit admiration and respect. The young entrepreneur realized that in order to accelerate her business even further she needed to take classes that enhanced her expertise and to be personally in charge of projects that required discipline, dedication, and respect.

### *Level Four: Corporate Boards*

This fourth and top level is where you find the "movers and shakers" of the business community, the top wage earners of the United States. When corporations look for "out-of-the box" solutions, they look for the caliber of people who inhabit this level. Those business owners who are invited to participate in the corporate boards are people who have all four levels of influence described above, likeable demeanor, ability to exercise authority, knowledge of reciprocal relationships, and strong personal power. Once you get to this level in the pyramid, you also receive compensation for your participation.

The leverage and amount of influence gained here is higher and more profitable than any of the other levels. It is at this point that you attract an incredible amount of social power and status *(the reward to attaining this level)*. You now enter into the elite and small social class of notable business owners in the United States.

You move up in this level like the prior one, acquiring a seat on the executive committee, then moving into the role of Board Chairman. While our young entrepreneur has not had this opportunity at this point, it is probably in her future.

By implementing the following recommendations, you too will accelerate your earning potential:

1) Show others that you care and are interested in their well-being.
2) Join a professional organization and volunteer to become part of the leadership team.
3) Learn to use the rule of reciprocity.
4) Analyze your current personal power and develop an action plan to increase it every day.

# NUGGET #15

## Organizations to Join For Successful Networking

### By Dr. Virginia Wells

Just imagine it is your first day as a business owner and you decide that today you are going to start *networking* to build your business. You researched the best ways to market your business and discovered that *networking* is the quickest and easiest way to build your business. So you get on the Internet to figure out the best place to network.

Your search for *networking* organizations gives you numerous organizations to pick from, but where do you start first? You ask yourself, "Which one of these organizations is going to promote my business so I get the fastest results?" You call up one of your business owner friends, who tells you that you need to join the local Chamber of Commerce. So is this the best place to start?

Stop! How do you know if the Chamber is going to be the best fit for you? Would you like to know the secret to selecting the organization that is right for you and your business? Here it is in a nutshell; there are five questions you need to answer…

Before I explain what those five questions are, let me share with you the five types of *networking* organizations you can join, so you have a better understanding of what you can choose from.

## *Chamber of Commerce*

The first type of organization that most business owners join when they open their business is their local Chamber of Commerce. However, there are different types of Chambers and for the purposes of this chapter, I am going to introduce you to two types of Chambers, your local Chamber and the ethnic Chambers. Chambers of Commerce are typically formed to provide business owners the opportunity to promote their business. Another benefit of joining a chamber is being able to form business relationships with other business owners.

The ethnic Chambers also make it possible for business owners to connect with corporations and city and government entities through their procurement opportunities. Some of these chambers have open membership; others may require you to be part of their ethnic group. Here are a few ethnic chambers that you might find in a large city:
- Asian Chamber of Commerce
- Black Chamber of Commerce
- Hispanic Chamber of Commerce
- Native American Chamber of Commerce

## *Industry/Trade organizations*

Industry or Trade organizations are the second type of *networking* group many people join. Business owners and professionals alike join this type of organization to stay informed on the most current trends in their particular industry. The focus of these organizations is to advocate for as well as educate their members about industry related issues and product ideas (which might enhance your product or service knowledge). They also serve as a place where their members can network. Membership usually requires connection to the industry in some way. These are a few industry and trade organizations:

- **American Institute of Certified Public Accountants (AICPA)**
  Address:        1211 Avenue of the Americas

New York, NY 10036
- Phone: 212-596-6200
- Website: www.aicpa.org

- **eMarketing Association**
  - Address: 224 Post Rd.
    #129
    Westerly, RI 02891
  - Phone: 800-496-2950
  - Website: www.emarketingassociation.com

- **Financial Planning Association**
  - Address: 1600 K Street NW
    Washington, D.C. 20006
  - Phone: 800-322-4237
  - Website: www.fpanet.org

- **Independent Insurance Agents & Brokers of America (IIABA)**
  - Address: 412 First Street S. E.
    Suite 300
    Washington, D.C. 20003
  - Phone: 202-86307000
  - Website: www.iiaba.org

- **The National Federation of Independent Business (NFIB)**
  - Address: 53 Century Blvd.
    Suite 250
    Nashville, TN 37214
  - Phone: 800-634-2669
  - Website: www.nfib.com

## *Professional women's organizations*

Let's say you decide that you want to narrow your focus to a smaller group of people, then look at your target audience. If your audience is primarily women, you could join the third type of networking organization, which is a professional women's organization. Yes, some of these organizations allow men to become members if their product or service is focused towards women.

Professional women's organizations have been traditionally formed to help women build their networks and create platforms to advance in their careers. Although there are numerous women's organizations to pick from, this is a sample for you to consider:

- **eWomenNetwork**
  Address: 14900 Landmark Boulevard
  Suite 540
  Dallas, TX  75254
  Phone: 972-620-9995
  Website: www.ewomennetwork.com

- **Heart Link**
  Website: www.heartlinknetwork.com

- **National Association for Executives (NAFE)**
  Address: 60 East 42nd Street
  Suite 2700
  New York, NY  10165
  Phone: 800-927-6233
  Website: www.nafe.com

- **National Association of Women Business Owners (NAWBO)**
  Address: 601 Pennsylvania Avenue NW South Building
  Suite 900
  Washington, D.C.  20004
  Phone: 800-556-2926
  Website: www.nawbo.org

- **The Joy of Connecting**
  Address: 1231 Bickham Way
  Smyrna, GA  30080
  Phone: 877-411-6611
  Website: www.thejoyofconnecting.com

*Professional business* **networking** *organizations*

By now you may have decided that you want to get laser-focused on driving business through *networking*. So consider joining the fourth type of *networking* organization, which is a professional business networking organization. These groups are limited in number of members in each chapter and they typically meet on a weekly basis. By meeting weekly, you have the opportunity to develop a business relationship faster and obtain personal referrals.

Exchanging referrals is the lifeblood of this type of organization, which is the upside to joining. The downside to becoming a member is that they normally only allow one person per business category to join, which eliminates the competition–at least in that group. These are some professional business *networking* organizations to consider:

- **BNI**
  Address: 545 College Commerce Way
  Upland, CA 91786
  Phone: 800-825-8286
  Website: www.bni.com

- **Hot Pink Mamas**
  Address: P. O. Box 33731
  Las Vegas, NV 89133
  Phone: 702-566-7465
  Website: www.hotpinkmamas.com

- **Leads Club**
  Address: P. O. Box 279
  Carlsbad, CA 92018
  Phone: 800-783-3761
  Website: www.leadsclub.com

- **LeTip International, Inc**
  Address: 4838 East Baseline Road
  Suite 123
  Mesa, AZ 85206
  Phone: 800-255-3847
  Website: www.letip.com

- ***Networking* For Professionals (NFP)**
  Phone: 212-227-6556

Website: www.networkingforprofessionals.com

## *Community Service Clubs*

Community Service Clubs are the fifth type of organization you can network in. The focus of these organizations is on creating fellowship and building a better community through volunteerism. Many of the organizations require the members to volunteer a certain number of hours per month for community projects. In this type of group you can demonstrate your civic involvement as well as your work ethic. By providing you a platform to improve your community, other members can see skills and competencies you possess that would go unnoticed otherwise. These are some of the largest community service clubs available:

- **Kiwanis International**
  - Address: 3636 Woodview Trace
    Indianapolis, IN 46268
  - Phone: 800-549-2647
  - Website: www.kiwanis.org

- **Lions Club International**
  - Address: 300 West 22nd Street
    Oak Brook, IL 60523
  - Phone: 630-571-5466
  - Website: www.lionsclubs.org

- **Optimist International**
  - Address: 4494 Lindell Blvd.
    St. Louis, MO 63108
  - Phone: 800-500-8130
  - Website: www.optimist.org

- **Rotary International**
  - Address: One Rotary Center
    1560 Sherman Avenue
    Evanston, IL 60201
  - Phone: 847-866-3000
  - Website: www.rotary.org

- **The Association of Junior League International Inc.**
  Address:    80 Maiden Lane
              Suite 305
              New York, NY 10038
  Phone:      212-951-8300
  Website:    www.ajli.org

Remember I told you that you needed to ask yourself five questions before you starting *networking*? Well, here they are:

1. **Product/Service**. What is the product or service that you are selling? (A product or service geared to business owners may be marketed more easily at a Chamber of Commerce, where more established businesses usually gather.)
2. **Target Market**. Who do you want as an ideal customer? An industry organization might be great to develop business relationships but it is unlikely that the people in your industry will be interested in purchasing products they perceive as "the competition." However, if your target market is women, you may find you have better success joining women's organizations (like eWomenNetwork) rather than your local Chamber of Commerce.
3. **Competition**. Who else is selling what you are selling? If you are in a very competitive industry you may find that joining a professional *networking* organization (like BNI) may suit your needs because they only allow one representative per type of business. This would allow you to find synergistic partners with whom you could share referrals.
4. **Competitive Advantage**. What makes your product or service unique or different? No matter which organization you join, you will have to introduce yourself and quickly state what it is you do and why you do it differently. Knowing what to say and what your competitive advantage is will make you appear confident in what you do. See the chapter on "60 Second Commercial Introductions" for the best way to do this.
5. **Marketing Strategies**: How are you getting the message out

about your business? It is critical to know how you plan to get the word out about your product and service, along with what marketing strategies you are going to use, <u>before</u> you go to *networking* events. The reason this is important is because you will be asked by people selling websites, advertising and printing companies to buy their services. You may find that some of them will make sense to purchase but knowing how you plan to market will ensure that you don't make a hasty decision–or an uninformed one.

By asking yourself these questions, you will discover which organization(s) is the best one for you to start *networking* in.

# NUGGET #16

## Using Social Media for Networking

### Introduction by Debra Pope

I met Ricci Neer as my roommate at an eWomenNetwork International Conference. She is vivacious, spunky, and smart. She was an eWomenNetwork Managing Director in El Paso, Texas and is now the Managing Director for the Austin, Texas Chapter.

She has a big heart and to illustrate this, one of our Managing Directors was diagnosed with breast cancer and unable to attend the conference. Ricci organized an impromptu rally to raise funds to buy t-shirts with words of encouragement on them, have our pictures taken wearing the shirts, and then sent them to the Managing Director as tangible evidence of our support.

I want Ricci on my team, and I'm glad to say she is. With her support, you are cheered on to success.

Her knowledge of social media is unparalleled. I'm thrilled to have her direct us into what I sometimes find a mystery, social media. I'm happy and grateful to have Ricci on this project.

Internet Fame Coach™ Ricci Neer works with smart, savvy professionals to help them successfully position themselves as experts in their fields. Starting out with a borrowed laptop on a dial-up Internet connection in 1999, Ricci shattered records with her business and soon became a corporate internet sales trainer. As the 2009 eWomenNetwork International Businesses Matchmaker of the Year award winner, Ricci has supported, connected and empowered over 5,000 clients and associates. She is co-host of The Shift Economy radio show and resides in Austin, Texas with her husband of 16 years. She has one son, three grown stepchildren and a menagerie of furbabies.

**Ricci Neer**
**Rock Star Media, LLC**
**262-757-8277**
**http://InspiredRockStar.com**

## Using Social Media for Networking

### By Ricci Neer

*"Transcendental marketing training and coaching for entrepreneurs, small businesses and independent professionals."*

If you are running a business or non-profit and wish to promote your offerings through online social media channels, keep in mind that your profile, comments, interactions and connections may be someone's first contact with you and your organization.

*Think about the prospect/customer experience. If they were to walk into your brick and mortar office or retail space, what would they feel, see and hear?*

Create your online space by putting careful thought into every aspect of the image you want to convey.

You are creating a virtual experience, so first and foremost, **be inviting**. The virtual platform is about transparency, openness and access.

*First impressions are emotional in nature. What kinds of things could you do to create a more positive virtual emotional impression?*

*What imagery would you like to convey to a potential client the moment they first connect with you online?*

After giving some thought as to how someone might experience your first encounter online, begin to think about your **virtual tour.**

A virtual tour gives your new potential business associate an overview and/or in-depth look at who you are and why they might want to stay connected with you or know more about you.

Oftentimes, during real-life *networking* events or times that we connect with others, we schedule coffee or lunch to get to know each other better. During this follow-up time, we exchange stories, share common ground and make decisions about how we might further our relationship.

Would you say it's true that when you "click" with someone based on personal connectedness, you have more interest in moving forward with a professional relationship? *(Know—like—trust...)*

*What might make someone "click" with you, on the internet, when you are not in a face to face situation?*

Think of your status updates, notes and interactions as "coffee talk". Be interesting and relatable.

Online communities not only make it easier to mimic your every day conversation, they also give you an opportunity to share months or even years of information and knowledge.

Which brings us to...your celebrity status.

People want to associate with and be connected to famous people...those who have made a difference, who are game changers, and who have accomplishments. People are looking for leaders.

There's a difference between being celebrity and being narcissistic. Consider actor, producer and rapper Will Smith. Smith understands the power of personal brand *(as well as the power of well-styled self-promotion)*.

Smith's first record was called "Big Willie Style". He set his intention to be "the biggest movie star in the world" during a time when he was on the verge of bankruptcy. When his films would open, he'd call them "big Willie weekend". "Willineum" was the name of his multi-platinum solo album.

Do you see a trend here? He knew that if he was to be unforgettable, he'd have to make a big splash, and that no one was going to do it for him.

Will Smith was consistently one Fortune magazine's Richest 40 under 40 —One of the forty wealthiest American's under forty years of age.

*If Will Smith was just getting started, and wanted to use the power of social media to build his brand, how do you think he'd do it?*

Will Smith would never ask "who cares what I have to say?" His mindset would be, "Y'all listen up—I've got something to say"...then he'd go on to make a difference, be memorable and do it "Big Willie" style!

## Nugget #16

*How much money and influence would you like to create by using social media to network?*

Let's take a look at someone who took a four million dollar retail business and turned it into a sixty million business, **in six years**, using social media.

Gary Vaynerchuk, who recently landed a seven-figure book deal, took over his family-owned liquor store in 2003. He started a daily podcast and soon became "internet famous."

*"By taking on established critics, using approachable terminology and promoting himself shamelessly, Vaynerchuk has become one of the online world's best-known faces, not to mention a rich man."* – SmartBrief on Entrepreneurs

Gary is internet famous, yet virtually unheard of in mainstream circles.

*Would becoming internet famous help you?*
*What could you accomplish by achieving internet fame?*

Create a persona that attracts people to want to know more about you and make that information easily found.

Even when you do develop a beneficial promotion strategy, there will still be people who take issue with it.

Just like in real life, only a small percentage of the people you meet are "your people". Focus your efforts on them. Your true friends will support you and be interested in your life.

What you offer is a gift that others are looking for. Whether it's your friendship, a connection, resource or wisdom, think of your presence on social media as a gift.

Keep in mind that other people are gifts also. This is why it's so important to engage.

It's also important that you blog. Blogging is a strategy attached to your social media plan.

It can be difficult to plan your blog in advance. Think about your blog as a work of contemporary art. Just get started and design it as you go.

Each time you make an entry, put a link to it on your social *networking* sites so that your connections can read about what you wrote. You are creating awareness and educating others.

Think creatively about your content. Make it exciting. How would you explain it at a party?

The web is a communications & media platform. Use it to become an authority whose opinions are respected.

The book "*Tribes*" by Seth Godin is based on the premise that there are individuals who are disenfranchised or dissatisfied with the status quo in your field and that you can rally those troops to create a loving and loyal community.

Gary Vaynerchuk did it with the wine community.

*Who is lost in your network?*
*What can you offer to create a community around it?*

Chris Brogan, co-author of "*Trust Agents*" says this about building community:
- Stand out
- Create a sense of belonging
- Leverage
- Develop access
- Develop an understanding of people (soft skills)
- Build mass

Power tips to keep in mind:

**Showcase your expertise, be aware of what tools or online channels people are using to form an impression of you, make others want what you've got and trust your opinion, leave a positive emotional impression, highlight those around you and make them rock stars, make people feel comfortable and build deep relationships, leverage relationships offline, empower your community to feel important, be in the center of your network and spread ideas, reach out to those who are up and coming, be visible and make an impact!**

When you spend time with a new connection, perhaps over

coffee, you share pieces of your life and create impressions with each other. On the internet, you don't have the verbal or facial cues during conversation.

*What might you be able to do to compensate and create an "overview" experience for new potential connections?*

Once you build momentum with a community, there's a huge value in staying connected to it. You'll want to stop by, smile, chat, catch people up and catch up with people on a regular basis.

*Can you see yourself being this involved with online communities?*

*What has to happen in order that you achieve success?*

During your time on the web, think about taking people on a journey. Take them to your events, your parties, let them peek inside your journal - leave behind something for others to remember as you go.

*What kinds of things could you do to take your friends along for the ride?*

*Perception is reality. If you could create your own virtual reality, what might that be?*

*What could you do to give people reasons to feel that they can trust you, that you are real, and authentic?*

Alan Graham, President of Mobile Loaves & Fishes (MLF), a homeless outreach in Austin, TX, uses social media for social good. His strategy was developed to:
- Change the paradigm of the way homelessness is viewed
- Empower people to become involved in service
- Position themselves as expert in the area of homelessness
- Influence elected officials
- Drive traffic to the website
- Multiply donations through a broad sustainable network.

You could create your strategy overview based on MLF's highly effective model.

*If someone were to ask, "What is your plan?" what would you say?*

# NUGGET #17

## Achieving & Maintaining Good Health for Successful *Networking*

### Introduction by Debra Pope

Because of 27 years in the airline and travel industry, then later in the fitness industry, I see an important analogy in what flight attendants say in their safety presentation just prior to takeoff: "Put on your oxygen mask first, then help others around you."

If you don't take care of your health first, you won't be around **or** you won't be **able** to do the things you want to do to help your friends, family and clients, or finish the legacy you leave behind. Without your health you have nothing. Unfortunately, most Americans spend more money on their cars' preventive maintenance than they do on their own preventive health.

I'm happy to report that this is changing, albeit more slowly than it should.

While *networking* is the way to build your business, you must pay attention to your health, even while Networking.

The nature of the food and beverages served at *networking* events can pose a possible threat to your nutrition and ultimately to your health. Many events are planned around food that is not a good nutritional choice.

Common fare at a *networking* event in the morning is pastries, donuts, and other high carbohydrate, processed foods. Many evening *networking* events offer food choices that are just as bad and include deep fried, bad-fat-filled appetizers. Finger foods tend to make it easier for *networking* participants to juggle plates, beverages and business cards. "Sit down" *networking* luncheons and dinners often include starchy, high carbohydrate foods and lots of high sugar and fat content desserts.

Like the other facets of *networking*, advance planning can keep you on track for maintaining good health. Be prepared when you head out the door of your home or office to attend a Networking event. Make sure you have eaten properly before going and aren't already starving and hungry.

1. **Don't Go to an Event Hungry** - Just like the advice about not going to the grocery store to shop for food when hungry, don't go to a *networking* event on an empty stomach. You'll be tempted to eat the donuts or pastries or fat-filled, deep fried appetizers if you do attend hungry.

2. **Take a Healthy Snack or Meal Alternative with You to the Event** - I take yogurt, fruit, hard-boiled eggs, a protein bar or a protein shake with me to the events I attend. It's best to be prepared in case only unhealthy choices are the only meal choices available.

3. **Don't Graze Mindlessly; Make Healthy Choices** - If you do go to a *networking* event with no way to have eaten before attending and no time to take a healthy snack or alternative with you, remember not to graze mindlessly while at the event. Research shows that people who eat fattening snacks or appetizers over a longer period of time can easily consume more than double the calories they consume during a regular meal.

4. **Don't Skip Your Work Out** - It's important to make sure you get in at least 3 workouts per week that include a combination of strength training and cardiovascular exercise

for optimum health. Schedule your work out on your calendar like an appointment with YOU! It's so important to get in your workouts, even with a busy work and *networking* schedule.

5. **Seek Out and Partner with a Doctor for Regularly Scheduled Check-Ups** – I'm happy to report that I've met and established trust in many of the doctors and health professionals I use for me and my family's health at *networking* events. I know them and have trust in them, and they know me because we've become friends through *networking*. I am dedicated to making sure to schedule yearly and regular check-ups with them for maintaining my and my family's optimum health.

Now, I'd like to introduce you to one of those doctors I met through *networking*. I met Dr. Skip Hart at an International eWomenNetwork Conference in Dallas several years ago. Not only is he my doctor, but he is a great, caring and wonderful friend. He's passionate about promoting health through proper nutrition, healthy lifestyle choices and natural, holistic medical treatments.

I'm happy to introduce Dr. Skip Hart, who will give you his valuable, unique perspective on staying healthy for, during and after *networking*.

"Dr. Skip" Hart, M.S., O.M.D, specializes in integrative healthcare and holistic nutrition. He completed the Oriental Medical Doctor's residency program through Conmaul's Oriental Medical Hospital in Seoul, South Korea, with an emphasis on women's health and infertility. His Oriental Medical Degree was completed at Florida College of Integrative Medicine in Orlando, Florida.

He is a Diplomate of the National Board of Naturopathic Medical Examiners. Dr. Skip has spent the last several years researching all forms of integrative medicine for such conditions as cancers and autoimmune disorders, as well as how wellness practices can aid in the prevention of disease.

Dr. Skip has an extensive background in natural medicine and has practiced and trained around the globe. His unique training in a long list of therapies allows him to give patients a true integrative health experience.

His focus is on wellness, anti-aging, ADD/ADHD, anxiety, depression, weight loss and the balancing of neurotransmitters. He utilizes Oriental Medicine as well as a myriad of other holistic methodologies in developing protocols and wellness programs at various companies and clinics in the United States.

With all this research and experience, Dr. Hart has been working with medical colleagues across the world to formulate a protocol and list of therapies and products that have sound backing and strong research to support their safety and efficacy.

**AskDrSkip.com, LLC**
**email: office@askdrskip.com**
**linkedin: www.linkedin.com/in/askdrskip**
**facebook: www.facebook.com/askdrskip**
**twitter: www.twitter.com/askdrskip**
**office: (972) 530-4609**

# Achieving & Maintaining Good Health for Successful *Networking*

### Dr. Skip Hart

Staying Healthy While *Networking* in a Toxic World…

I think the best way to begin my section of the book, especially as it relates to the *networking* aspect, is to tell you the story of how I met my dear friend, Debra Pope. It was the summer of 2008 and I was traveling with my partner to New Delhi, India with a group called Vitamin Angels to help oversee and distribute Vitamin A in remote villages to help treat and prevent blindness in children.

Any of you who have been to, or seen anything related to, India will attest to the fact that India is one big and very overwhelming country, especially in the major metropolitan cities. We were scheduled to travel from New Delhi to Varanasi. Varanasi is one of the oldest known and continually inhabited cities in the world and is regarded as the most holy city to the Hindus. Exhausted from our extensive plane rides and travels across India, we finally arrived in Varanasi. We, of course, stopped off at the Taj Mahal, even though it was a little out of our way.

This extra jaunt did not help with the fatigue by compounding all the travel in such a short time. We were slated to be in the city for several weeks and were still ill-equipped, despite of all our preparations before leaving the states. We settled into our work with the children and adjusted to a very different life while in India. This trip was life-changing to say the least.

It was in Varanasi that we met Marilyn Tam. Many of you may know her from the eWomenNetwork, as well as, from the Glow Project and her work with the clinic HealthWalk. I hold HealthWalk very dear to my heart because I have personally witnessed profound results from using products created by their company. Having the incredible pleasure of spending time with this amazing woman after I had traveled across the world and by sheer happenstance ran into at the same hotel we were staying at, was such amazing synchronicity. I learned that she was also there with the Vitamin Angels group, but this is where the story really gets interesting!

Marilyn and I had so many similar interests we became fast friends within the intense experience that is anyone's first trip to India. We exchanged emails and phone numbers and as our trip to India was coming to a close, committed to remain in contact. After returning to the states, I was so awe-struck at the quality of the company and health products that she co-founded and visioneered that I called her a few weeks later and arranged to fly San Diego to see her again and explore her clinic.

After we left India, and before heading back to Dallas, we decided since we were on that side of the world we might as well fly to Nepal and visit Kathmandu. While in India there was a considerable adjustment period, especially with our hotel accommodations. They were much different than we were accustomed to back in the United States. When we arrived in Nepal and got settled in our hotel room, I was in the bathroom and was ecstatic that: 1. Toilet paper was readily available and 2. Toilet paper was perforated. In the same instance that this wave of excitement washed over us regarding the perforation of the toilet paper, we quickly realized how out of whack our priorities were if we were so happy about toilet paper. This brief foray into my story regarding the toilet paper is to hopefully remind you to not take things so seriously and not take anything for granted in your life. Life is too precious and much too short. Many millions of people in India and in the United States have nothing tangible and are very happy. Truly look at your life and what is important to you and to your family. Please live in the now and be in the moment. In the words of the author Dr. Richard Carlson, "Don't sweat the small stuff…and it's all small stuff!"

After the HealthWalk clinic visit, I returned home to Dallas, and who did I receive a telephone call from, but Mrs. Marilyn Tam, informing me she was going to be in Dallas. Ecstatic to see her again, we made plans to catch up and have dinner after the annual eWomenNetwork Conference.

While at the conference assisting with the manning of the HealthWalk table, who should approach us out of the thousands of women and start up a conversation, but the *networking* Diva extraordinaire, Debra Pope. After a few short minutes of instant connection we quickly realized that out of all these people present at the conference we had offices literally several doors down from each other in the same town and had never met before. What a small world we live in and how amazing the experiences are when we open our eyes and see, as in the teaching of Carl Jung and Deepak Chopra, the synchronicity life sends to us in every moment.

This story is pivotal because it was Debra who ushered me, gently kicking and screaming, into the world of *networking*. Mind you now, my expertise is in the medical field, namely holistic and alternative medicine, and not in marketing or business. My relationship with Debra has evolved from that of a business acquaintance to one of a deep friendship. I am constantly running in a multiplicity of directions at a hundred miles per hour. She always manages to be there for me, rein me in and help keep me in the loop of building relationships with an endless array of amazing people – be they in eWomenNetwork or otherwise. Debra is one amazing person and has been an invaluable asset in helping to build relationships and subsequently my business.

It is with Debra's patience and kindness that I have had the privilege to have a venue in which to teach people some amazing health and wellness strategies, since so many people are crying out for something other than a prescription bottle from their medical doctor. I am not speaking poorly of medical doctors or pharmaceutical drugs. In general, however, they are ill-equipped to deal with the vast numbers of chronic degenerative diseases that are becoming ever-present in our society and world at large. There are so many wonderful things in the conventional field that "natural" medicine is not equipped to deal with, and vice versa.

In my holistic health care practice, my passion is to educate patients with chronic degenerative and often debilitating diseases —to take them to the root of their disease process, discover its origin and teach my clients the tools with which to begin to heal. Facilitating a positive change in peoples' lives, as well as influencing the current state of medicine in our culture's healthcare system is, and continues to be, my primary focus.

It is with great pleasure that I am able to present to you the following tips for staying healthy while *networking* (and at home) in a fast-paced, stressful environment, where it is easier to make unhealthy food choices. Making the shift to a healthy lifestyle does not have to be difficult but it does take some work and adjustments.

**Food!**

The old and very clichéd adage "you are what you eat" is so true. I spend countless hours educating clients on the importance of food and their dietary habits. The various types of food that we put into our bodies make the biggest impact on our overall health.

In addition, food causes other issues that affect millions of Americans. These include bowel issues, such as constipation and diarrhea, or any of the other myriad of related conditions, such as GERD, heartburn, bloating, gas, belching, etc. It is not uncommon for us to see a commercial touting the newest medication to help prevent the upset stomach we get from consuming the double meat, double cheeseburger and fries. Now most of us, including me, love a good hamburger and fries. Never mind that this traditional American meal is one of the worst possible food combinations we can eat.

As a rule, especially when you are dealing with issues in your health related to your gastrointestinal tract, proteins and carbohydrates should be separated and not consumed together. I realize that this is a very "odd" concept for most folks to grasp, but one that I have seen that makes a huge difference in the lives of many of the people I consult.

Most of us have a tendency to consume, on average, the same 30 foods 80% of the time. This consistency leads to many problems with food allergies and sensitivities. These problems pop up in some very common places: our immune system as well as our intestinal tracts.

In the past it was common for us to eat with the seasons. This is no longer the case. We can eat the same fruits and vegetables all year round. This also assists in the consistency of eating the same foods over and over. Rotate your diet. Food variety in your diet really is the "spice of life." This rotation will decrease the immune system's response against what it perceives as foreign invaders and allow your body to heal. Food sensitivities and allergies can lead to issues such as headaches, acid reflux, diarrhea, constipation, learning disorders, ADD/ADHD, celiac disease, autoimmune disorders…the list goes on and on.

Just because the overweight guy in the antacid commercial can eat the double cheeseburger with fries certainly doesn't mean you should. Acid reflux and heartburn are just some of the subtitles of symptoms your body is, in actuality, SCREAMING at you. It is telling you that something is not right. Listen to your body; it knows you. Do what it says. You can still eat fun stuff and not deprive yourself. In making healthier choices you will have quality and longevity in your life and health. I know personally, I do not want longevity without quality of life.

Things that should be reduced and even eliminated from our diets altogether are all processed and pre-packaged foods, anything laden with chemicals, pesticides, food coloring, additives, monosodium glutamate (MSG), all dairy products, hormone and antibiotic rich meats, artificial sweeteners, and frankly, anything you cannot pronounce. If you cannot pronounce it, you probably shouldn't be putting into your body. That also goes for anything you may be putting **on** your body, such as personal care products like soaps, shampoos, hair gels, make-up and toothpaste. This is especially important in children. Babies are constantly exposed to an overload of dangerous products at birth. Our skin is our largest organ, and please do not think for one second that your skin does not absorb and send directly into your bloodstream anything and everything you put on it.

Main foods to minimize (or buy from a source that you know processes their meat in a healthy manner) for a multitude of reasons, including hormones and antibiotics being added to them, are products like all dairy, poultry and any red meat products, corn, wheat, gluten, refined sugar and flour. There are many studies out there that show the decrease in effectiveness of our immune system for several hours after consuming the smallest amounts of sugar.

If your stomach or health seems to be giving you issues and you cannot figure out the cause, there is a simple test that can be run whereby your blood is tested against about 100 foods and the severity of the reaction is measured. This is called a food sensitivity test. With the results of the tests, the exact culprits can be removed from the diet and your health can be regained by removing the stressors and allowing the intestinal tract to repair. Then foods which were once problematic can be reintroduced slowly over a period of a few weeks. If no symptoms are noticed then a moderate amount of them may remain in your diet.

*Should I eat organic food and what difference will it make?* I am asked this question frequently. It is usually followed by the quip, "I would love to eat organic, but it is so expensive." In a perfect world I would say YES, eat all organic, buy everything ranging from your food, soaps, lotions, potions, shampoos and conditioners to eco-friendly cleaners and clothes from a health food or eco-friendly store.

There is a tremendous benefit from eating organic food. It is grown and processed without the use of harmful chemicals and pesticides. Improving your health by changing your diet is probably the most profound tidbit of information I could ever teach you. Take these words not only to your heart, but also to your lips. Additionally, most organic farmers utilize soil that is rich in minerals and is in much better shape nutritionally than its conventional counterparts. Conventional soil is often so depleted that it yields crops that are "nutritionally dead." This makes for no real value for your body or health. My advice is to eat organic as much as you can and utilize the products and cleaners that you can, as much and as often as is feasible for you, both financially, and for your health.

By doing whatever you can afford to do, you are still taking a huge, stressful burden off your immune system. Every little bit that you do will make a huge difference to your body. With decreasing this ever-increasing toxic burden, you are allowing your body to have a chance to work on healing itself. When we constantly bombard our delicate systems with food, cleaners, alcohol, tobacco, drugs and all the toxicity life has to offer, which has no nutritional value and is loaded with toxic chemicals, our systems begin to deteriorate. By making the choice and the shift to organic and health food, you are making a decision not only for your health, but also as a consumer. With your money, you are voting. You are helping to drive down the cost of these extremely beneficial foods in the grocery store. This is economics 101. Supply versus demand. This will eventually allow the masses to access organic products at a lower, more affordable cost. Unfortunately, for many people health food is price-pointed right out of their budgets.

While you are at a *networking* event things to consider are minimizing or eliminating your consumption of carbohydrates by choosing the protein. Eat more salad and vegetables. Choose fruit instead of the desert. Avoid fried foods at all costs. Bringing a protein bar from home is also an option.

Quick Tips: Eat relaxed and not rushed, never standing. Eat with friends and family. Chew your food and eat slowly. Don't eat big, animal protein-laden meals past 8:30 pm. Eat smaller meals more frequently. If you must use salt, use a high quality, mineral rich sea salt product. When you eat breakfast, focus on eating proteins and not carbohydrates and lastly, for goodness sake: do not overeat!

Overeating is right up there with one of the worst things you can do to your digestive system. This decreases enzyme activity and greatly reduces your body's ability to digest your food and when it cannot digest, all that food just sits in your colon and putrefies.

There is a documentary on food that I highly recommend you watch. It is called "Food Inc." This movie will further your understanding of just how important it is for you to know what you are eating and where it is coming from. The filmmakers did an extraordinary job of laying out the facts on the positives and negatives from both a health perspective and a humanitarian perspective in relation to the animals and economics of the food and agriculture industry.

**Water**

Most folks are chronically dehydrated. Did you know that most hunger pains are actually a sign that body needs water and not food?

Regarding the ever popular bottled water question, I have spent countless hours researching the issue of filtering water, as well as bottled water. My advice is to use a good quality filter on the taps in your home. Most importantly, your showers and bathtubs should have water filters. In the shower you absorb more chemicals than in the water you drink from the tap. This is because your largest organ, your skin, is totally exposed, absorbing all the chemicals and fumes from the water in a heated, vapor state. This drives those toxins right into our systems. Any minimization of chemical exposure is helpful to all the systems in your body, ranging from your respiratory tract to your liver.

There are many reputable companies that make water filters. Do not go overboard here. Drink out of glass containers whenever possible. Do not store plastic water bottles in your car, especially in the summer. Do not reuse and refill disposable plastic water bottles. Use bottles that are stainless steel or from plastic that is (Bisphenol-A) BHP free. We are attempting to give the body a reduction in exposure to the chemicals in the plastics, which tend to leach into the water at warmer temperatures.

Decrease and eliminate your intake of soda drinks, coffee, juices and anything containing high fructose corn syrup. There are lots of marketing materials being released about the safety of this—

please opt for products containing no added sugar (and certainly NO artificial sweeteners) or made with real cane sugar instead. Your body will thank you for it. Increase your intake of high quality, well-filtered water. I prefer you drink spring water – stay away from distilled water, as it is no longer alive and devoid of minerals that your body is already most probably lacking. There is a great product that "optimizes" your water called Hydromag. Using water which has been Hydromag'd in my shakes and throughout my day is an invaluable part of my personal routine and protocol.

While *networking*—and throughout your day, in general—it is imperative that you consume enough water. Choose water over sugar-laden carbonated beverages. Drink unsweetened iced tea without artificial sweeteners. Drinking plenty of good quality water is going to help you feel full, so your tendency to overeat will be drastically reduced. Reduce and/or eliminate alcohol, as well.

**Food Storage and Cookware**

I realize you could very easily and quickly get overloaded with all the suggestions I am making. Please take baby steps. These implementations and changes will help make cumulative, long lasting beneficial effects on your health.

Do not store your leftovers in plastic. Use a glass version with a rubber lid. These are widely available. When you store food in plastic, it is absorbing all the unwanted toxins. These chemicals found in the plastic have been shown to affect hormone levels of both men and women, not to mention the cellular and DNA damage that can occur. Never heat your food up in the microwave in a plastic dish or by covering it with plastic wrap.

Again, this is just making an amalgamation of chemical soup. Do you really want to eat food that is contaminated with melted plastics? As if the meats and foods we are currently eating aren't tainted enough with hormones, pesticides, herbicides, and antibiotics.

Microwaves are fine to use for short bursts to heat up your food only. Never cook your food in the microwave. Avoid using the microwave whenever possible. Use the oven or toaster oven whenever possible to minimize the food's and your body's exposure to the microwaves.

Cookware is a very different issue. Please do not use anything that is non-stick coated. This technology, while very helpful with clean-up, is not so good from a health perspective. Any of my readers who are bird owners know that you cannot use non-stick cookware with birds in the house. The fumes those pans emit while cooking will kill the bird, much like the canaries that were sent in the coal mines before the miners.

I know that we are not birds. The harsh reality is if it's not safe for birds, then it is certainly not safe for humans. If it is killing the birds, what is it doing to our bodies? We are living in a world where cardiovascular disease, cancers and many other very serious illnesses are running rampant.

There are a few companies which I have found to have safe cookware. It can be as simple as using stainless steel. They are slightly more labor intensive to clean but much healthier for your body than the alternative of using an easy to clean pan and absorbing all the toxins from non-stick coated cookware.

**Exercise**

Exercise is not something that you will be doing during a *networking* event but it is important to "look the part" and be a picture of health, regardless of your profession! It would be very difficult for me to promote weight loss if I was obese–which I was. This is not healthy in any capacity. People would not have taken me seriously if I was trying to teach weight loss while I was overweight myself. Perception from your potential clients could be the difference between you closing or losing the sale. Being a proper weight is important not only for business but also for your overall health.

Exercise need not be a big deal…get off your fanny and get your body moving and sweating. Walking, rebounding on a trampoline, swimming, yoga and Pilates are all great forms of exercise. This is important for your stress management, mental health and physical health, as well as the health of your lymphatic system. Exercise also helps to increase your bowel movements and any of you that spend any time with me know that healthy bowel habits are extremely important to me. Exercise tends to be the first thing that goes from our routine when life gets in the way. The opposite should be the case. We should continue or start exercising when "the going gets tough," especially when we are ill or diagnosed with a new illness, which is when so many people discontinue this practice. Please consider continuing or starting an exercise practice especially in these instances, as the positive effects are overwhelming. Remember, it does not have to be painful. Walking for 15-30 minutes daily, especially after meals, is invaluable to your health. By helping to reduce stress and improve your muscle tone, you will have the energy and gumption to hit the proverbial *networking* "ground" running and garner that business that we all so desperately want.

**Bio-Identical Hormone Balancing (BHRT)**

This is extremely important for both women and men. I see mostly women for this, and they tend to not be shy about being proactive about seeking help when something is out of balance. Women will start to notice vaginal dryness, breast tenderness, mood swings, hot flashes, etc., and they immediately seek out help. Men do not so readily seek out help when issues with their bodies arise, such as fatigue, increased abdominal fat, diminishing sex drive and hair loss, just to rattle off a few symptoms. It is important that you have your hormone levels checked—and then utilize a protocol to optimize those levels. There are many beneficial, natural and holistic methods that can be employed to correct these imbalances.

Not only can there be an improvement of symptoms to our bodies, there are tremendous amounts of research out there that show by having optimal levels of hormones, issues such as diabetes, cardiovascular disease, and several forms of cancer may be prevented. This is a win-win situation all around. By making sure your hormones are balanced, you will feel better, have increased energy and improved skin tone, which will make you feel fresh and vivacious, and your networking group, clients and friends will all want to know what you are doing to be looking and feeling so good. When you seek assistance, whether it is with me or another practitioner, please insist on Bio-Identical products and not their synthetic counterparts. The health benefits are obtained when using Bio-Identical Hormones.

## Stress Management/Relaxation Response/Meditation

Meditation and/or relaxation techniques are the primary key for your overall health and hormonal balance, as well as helping to manage your stress, anxiety and depression.

Whatever you want to call it–prayer, meditation, stress management or a relaxation technique–it is vital to your overall health and wellness. We live in a world where everything must be done yesterday. You check your email, voicemail, text messages, faxes, and your Facebook page every second from your smartphone. I am just as guilty as the next person. It is imperative for everyone to spend a few dedicated moments each day to focus on eliciting a relaxation response.

There is a great little book called *"The Relaxation Response"* by Herbert Benson, M.D. that very clearly and very simply explains the medical benefits, as well as easy relaxation principles and techniques you can employ into your daily routine. He also explains the conventional science and research that has been done in regard to the proven health benefits of managing your stress in this manner.

There are improvements in cardiovascular disease, sleep improvement, hormone balancing and general quality of life improvement when these methods are introduced into your routine. This must be done in addition to your exercise regime.

A very simple method to help with relaxation and stress is to find a quiet spot in your home. Please use the same spot each time, if possible. Light a candle or burn some incense. This technique helps to train the brain to relax. As you get into the habit, over a period of time the brain will eventually begin to relax when lighting any candle or burning incense. Smells are very powerful for the brain. Be sure to select a relaxing scent such as lavender. Close your eyes and focus on your breathing. Breathe in through your nose and out through your mouth. Take deep, slow, and consistent breaths. I also recommend you use a saying—it can be anything uplifting. I often recommend that my clients use the term "Infinite Love and Gratitude." This is a recommendation from the title of the book "The Power of Infinite Love and Gratitude" by Dr. Darren Weisman. It is a very powerful mantra, if you will. This is used to help change and chase away any thoughts you may have during the relaxation exercise.

Please do not beat yourself up with the stress of "I cannot clear my mind" or "I am having too many thoughts and I cannot meditate!" These thoughts are part of what make you who you are. It is not about getting rid of them. It is about you taking control of the thoughts that have control of you. If the thoughts come flooding in while meditating, such as "I need to do the laundry" or "I have to clean the house," gently bring your thoughts back to the mantra "Infinite Love and Gratitude." The repetition of the manta is not meant to be forced. This is a gentle process whereby you see the mantra in your mind, much like an electronic sign in your brain. If you find yourself "thinking," gently go right back to the mantra. The decrease in frequency of the thoughts will come in time with the practice. Be patient. It's a virtue!

What could be better than Infinite Love and Gratitude, I ask you? That is some powerful stuff. Relax on that thought for a while, and little else will matter. There is a lot to be said about changing your thoughts to change your life. It can be done. With a positive attitude, the world is your oyster. Having positive thoughts guiding your life... What could be better? Please read the book "*Excuses Be Gone*" by Dr. Wayne Dyer. It will change your life and the way you think.

This freedom from your excessive thoughts, stresses, anxiety, and depression can be yours. You just have to make a commitment to utilize the techniques to help you relax. It is a cumulative process. The benefits are seen over a period of time. This is why it should not be discontinued. You will also notice a general difference in the way you respond to the stressors in your day when you have a consistent relaxation practice in place.

Recap for Relaxation Technique:

1. Pick a relaxing spot. Use it consistently.
2. Light a candle or burn incense.
3. Close your eyes and focus on your breathing.
4. Use anything uplifting – a prayer of your choosing or the saying "Infinite Love and Gratitude."
5. Do this technique at LEAST once daily, preferably two times per day, early morning and before the sun sets. Do not attempt to do it before bed as it can interfere with your sleep.

If you fall asleep during the meditation, that is totally fine. Your body undoubtedly needed the rest. Honor that and move on. With your practice you will find that you will not fall asleep after a period of time has elapsed. As with anything in life, "practice makes perfect." Please do not give up. This is a lifelong commitment that will yield many very positive outcomes.

Do not over-think the process here. It is that easy. Good luck! One additional caveat here, and that is meditation is not a religious technique. Please do not let the verbiage scare you if meditation is a foreign word. It is exactly the same principle if you input a "prayer" instead of a "mantra." Many of my friends and clients use things like the Lord's Prayer or the Rosary. It makes no difference. Make it more like an exercise, make it more spiritual or religious—it is totally up to you. Neither way is right nor wrong. It will all ultimately give you the same positive outcomes in the end. Do the method that feels best to you.

Obviously a meditation is not something you will be performing during a *networking* event. However, by having this as part of your daily routine, your sleep will improve, energy levels will increase, and stress will be reduced. These are all things that will laser-sharpen our edge, which in the business world will make us more competitive so we can get out there and hit the ground running and show the world what we are made of.

## Conclusion

Dear readers,

Thank you so much for your precious time and attention. My passion has always been, and continues to be, to get information out to as many people as I can who have questions about their health and who need alternatives to conventional medical wisdom. I love conventional medicine. It is not about separation with me; it is about unity and integration. Both disciplines of medicine have their place. We need to account for the fact that there are better decisions we should be making in regard to our health. These decisions can be made in an educated vein when you have the information you need in front of you to help you come to your conclusions. I hope I have met my objectives.

Most people I meet are desperately searching for something "else." They are tired of not feeling well; they are tired of being sick and tired of being on tons of medications. I have spent the bulk of my career searching for answers to the questions asked so frequently in complementary and alternative medicine. What works, what doesn't? It is these pearls that I offer to you, my family, clients, friends and readers. I thank all of you from the bottom of my heart who made my contribution to this book possible. I love you all more than my words can express. You all have always been, and continue to be, my inspiration and drive for doing what I do.

Whether your business is in the financial field or medical field, it is imperative that you stay healthy. This will ensure that you will be able to do the things you love and grow your network of business colleagues and friends while being free from aches, pains, cancers and heart disease.

If you have any questions regarding staying healthy in a crazy, toxic world or if you have questions regarding anything you have read, please feel free to contact my office in the Dallas Metro area. I have researched and in most cases personally used what I recommend. I am available for consultations, concierge services, seminars and lectures.

Disclaimer: These statements have not been evaluated by the Food and Drug Administration. The products, services, therapies, education and information presented here is not intended to diagnose, treat, cure or prevent any disease. If you are pregnant, nursing, taking medication, or have a medical condition, consult your physician before implementation of any products, services or therapies. No guarantees are expressed or implied.

# NUGGET #18

## The Fortune Is In The Follow-Up. It Takes Time, Talent, and Tenacity To Get To The Treasure!

By Debra Pope

With focused attention to this last Nugget, your quest for meaningful friendships, deep fulfilling referral partner relationships and devoted clients will be assured. Follow-up "seals the deal."

The saying "Rome wasn't built in a day" illustrates that time and effort must be expended to build something lasting and meaningful. Rome was built one stone at a time, with an investment of time, effort and resources carefully planned and placed. You need to look at *networking* with the same approach.

Many of us have high expectations that by attending a *networking* event or two we will instantly strike gold! We have expectations that we'll meet those dream friends and clients immediately with just a few minutes of time and effort expended, and everything will be perfect! We'll think we'll immediately sell thousands of dollars of our products and services and never need to do anything again to promote ourselves and our business

In a perfect world the stars and planets will align and voila! We can attend an event we'll strike it rich!

My goal is not to burst the bubble of the expectations you may have for your *networking*, but to provide you with tools and knowledge to make the investment of time and money be well spent.

My goal is to arm you with the tools to mine the gold that is available to you through focused, intentional, relationship-building *networking*.

Just like a miner digging or panning for gold, you have to keep at it, paying attention to the smallest details. Just like the miner who knows that the gold is there, you know you have to keep at it because "it takes time, talent and tenacity to get to the treasure."

The mistake some people make is to race through events, grabbing as many cards as possible, not making any real connection with anyone. They may assume that there is value in numbers and they want to make as many contacts as possible.

The truth is that at each *networking* event you attend, you can expect to meet three to four business people that you "click" with or feel a warm connection with. Then, you can expect that you may meet another six to eight people who made an impression on you, but you didn't have the time to really form a connection.

To make the most of the time and money spent to attend the event, follow-up is a must! Categorize the cards you received while at the event as soon as possible after the *networking* event.

**Categorize the business cards you've received as a #1, #2, or #3.**

> **Category #1** - The #1's will be the three or four people you want to give the highest priority, those with whom you will want to concentrate on forming a continuing relationship as a friend, referral partner or prospective client.
>
> **Category #2** - These will be the people you want to follow up with, but you aren't sure about because of shortage of time.
>
> **Category #3** - The #3's are the people you see who have potential, who you will want to add to your database, but may or may not be a future friend, referral partner or customer.

Just as all the previous Nuggets are necessary components of insuring successful *networking*, last but absolutely not least is "***the fortune is in the follow-up***".

Research shows that you must have multiple contacts with a prospective customer or client before a sale or transaction will take place.

Everyone needs to buy, but nobody wants to be "sold." The only way to successfully build trust and business relationships is through follow-up. Follow-up is imperative to form the relationship and to keep it alive. To have growth in a business relationship, follow-up is equal to planting a plant and providing sufficient sunshine and consistent watering after planting.

Below are suggested methods of follow-up for you to use after you have met prospective clients through *networking*. Some are obvious, but some of the follow-up methods may be new to you.

**Follow Up Methods and Who to Follow Up With Are:**

**Email** - #1, #2, and #3 Card Categories

**Telephone Call** - #1 and #2 Card Categories

**Schedule a One On One Meeting** - #1 Card Category

**Personal Card or Letter by US Mail** - #1 and #2 Card Categories

**Send Invitation to Your Upcoming Events** - #1, #2 and #3 Card Categories

**Add To Your Database for Direct Contact Advertising** - #1, #2, and #3 Card Categories

**Email Follow Up:**

I recommend you follow up with a personal email within 24 hours of meeting for all three categories of people you've met at a Networking event. However, an email alone will not be enough to build a relationship with this person. You must take the next step for future follow up.

**Telephone Call:**

After you've sent an email, within 48 hours of meeting the person, call the Category #1 prospects. Let them know you enjoyed meeting them and would love to set up a one-on-one meeting with them to learn more about their business. Make no sales pitch about what you offer, but instead, let the person know you want to learn about them and how you can support them in **their** business. Part of the purpose of the telephone call will be to set up a one-on-one Meeting with them. The one-on-one appointment should be kept to no more than a one hour meeting and this parameter should be set as you make the appointment with them.

**One-On-One Meeting:**

For your #1 Category cards, schedule the one-on-one meeting. The meeting could be at your office or theirs, or a public place like a coffee shop, upbeat deli or restaurant with an upscale cocktail lounge for appetizers and beverages.

No sales pitch is appropriate at the beginning of this one–on-one meeting. The beginning of the meeting should be devoted to a fact finding mission to confirm if this person is a good fit for you as a referral partner to send your clients, friends or family to. Use leading questions to get to know the person. Ask the person to tell you about themselves and their business. Ask them how you can support them in their business. Toward the end of the meeting, make an offer to tell them about your business and what you can do for them.

**Personal Thank You Note Card by US Mail:**

Do this for your #1 Category cards. More than ever before, a personal follow-up thank you card is appreciated. It shows your interest in a business relationship and shows your care and concern for others. It shows that you are a person of substance and professionalism to take the time to send a card.

Attractive note cards and thank you cards are available in many stores and office supply chains, but the system I prefer to use is an online card design and contact system called Send Out Cards, where a "real" card is mailed from the Send Out Cards headquarters by the

US Mail.

Send Out Cards allows you to import contacts from your database lists into their database. You design your own cards using your logo and/or picture or use others that area already designed in the Send Out Cards catalog. Send Out Cards even allows you to use a font that is in your own handwriting.

Send Out Cards has an internal tracking system of when you sent the card and even a photocopy of text included in the type of card that went to the person. Each time you send a card to that person, it's recorded by Send Out Cards

You can set up groups of the types of mailings you want to do, such as Christmas card group, Birthday group, Thank You group, or any type of group you want to do a mailing to. You can set the cards up to go out on a specific date.

Once you have taken these steps to follow up to form relationships with the business people you wish to pursue, you must continue to contact them through e-mail, telephone calls, cards, invitations to your events, and your direct contact advertising.

In a simple way, it brings me to what my mom has always told me: "To have a friend, you have to be a friend."

Never forget that the fortune is in the follow-up!

## About the Author

Debra Pope is from a small rural community in Missouri. She attended Truman State University.

She had a successful career for over 20 years in the airline and travel agency industry. She was with Eastern Airlines in Sarasota, Florida, then later in travel agency management. She founded, owned and managed three travel agencies in Missouri, as well as a Missouri state licensed vocational school training travel agents.

After her travel industry career Debra entered the fitness industry and founded, owned and managed seven women's fitness centers in North Texas.

She is an Executive Managing Director with eWomenNetwork, an international women's organization based in Dallas, Texas,.
Through Networking, she has successfully made hundreds of business to business introductions for professionals to meet, build relationships and do business.

Debra and her husband Paul have four grown children. Her favorite author is Mark Twain. Debra's favorite saying is, "The best way to predict your future is to create it!"

Contact Information

**Debra K. Pope**
**Networking for Novices,**
debra@networkingfornovices.com
214-592-5196

# NETWORKING FOR NOVICES